THE DEPARTMENT CHAIR PRIMER
Leading and Managing Academic Departments

Don Chu
University of West Florida

ANKER PUBLISHING COMPANY, INC.
Bolton, Massachusetts

The Department Chair Primer

Leading and Managing Academic Departments

ISBN 1-882982-93-2

Composition by Beverly Jorgensen, Studio J Graphic Design
Cover design by Jennifer Arbaiza Graphic Design

Anker Publishing Company, Inc.
563 Main Street
P.O. Box 249
Bolton, MA 01740-0249 USA

www.ankerpub.com

Library of Congress Cataloging-in-Publication Data

Chu, Donald.
  The department chair primer : leading and managing academic departments / Don Chu.
      p. cm.
  Includes bibliographical references and index.
  ISBN 1-882982-93-2
  1. Departmental chairmen (Universities) 2. Universities and colleges—Departments. I. Title.
  LB2341.C543 2006
  378.1'11—dc22
                                     2005021976

To my wife Janine, who,
through life's thick and thin,
has given me her loyalty,
commitment, and love.

TABLE OF CONTENTS

About the Author

Don Chu is dean of the College of Professional Studies at the University of West Florida. He earned his BA from Oberlin College, and his MA in sociology and Ph.D. in education from Stanford University. Professor Chu has written and edited five books and numerous articles on higher education, sports, and the Olympic Games. From 1988–1998 he chaired the Department of Kinesiology at California State University–Chico and served as consultant for chair affairs in the Office of the Provost from 1998–1999. He was the California State University (CSU) System Executive Fellow in the Office of the Chancellor in 1999–2000, and completed the Harvard Management Development Program. Working in collaboration with the CSU Statewide Academic Senate, the Office of the Chancellor, and Dr. Sally Veregge, he conducted the 20-campus CSU Department Chair Survey (2002) and wrote the associated report. He is the founder of Academic Leadership Consulting and can be reached at dchu@uwf.edu.

PREFACE

Chairs are fond of saying that they are between a rock and a hard place. As middle-level managers they take fire from both sides of the frontline. What chairs should know first, however, is that the present realities of higher education place almost every manager and leader between diverse, sometimes conflicting, constituent groups. Administrators at all levels of the university and college are being asked to do more with less, and to prove that that is the case. Navigating academic units through difficult times requires the sensitivity of an artist, the quantitative skills of an accountant, the vision of a scout on constant reconnaissance, and a moral philosopher's sense of what is right. In this primer, I have tried to concisely convey some of the ideas that have already worked for chairs. Every campus is so different, and every department so individual, however, that no claim can be made for universal applicability for all of the ideas contained in this book. What I do claim is that some of these ideas will help most department chairs in the course of their difficult work.

While researching this book, visits were made to campuses from Alaska to Florida, New England to San Diego, and almost all of the 23 campuses that comprise the California State University (CSU) System. One of the most important facts of American higher education is how individual each school is. To wit, despite the fact that the CSU System has a standard faculty union contract, the particular history, culture, economics, politics, and sociology of each campus renders universally applicable theory impossible. Readers are encouraged to pick and choose what will work for them in their idiosyncratic situations. Many of the ideas presented in this primer are not mine; they come from chairs just like those reading this handbook. These are ideas that have worked for department administrators and that might work for other chairs who find themselves in similar circumstances.

A good deal of theory is left out of this text. Readers are encouraged to look at the work of Hecht, Higgerson, Gmelch, and Tucker (1999) for the bigger picture. In this book, just enough background has been presented to set the context for the suggestions in each chapter so that chairs will know they are not alone in the problems they face.

Academic leadership and management are both art and science. While research has been used to inform the contents of these pages, most of this book's focus is drawn from the practical experiences of former and current department chairs. The length of this book is itself admission to the overriding reality of department chairing—that there is too little time to do too much. The organization of this primer is based on what chairs have said they do and what they need to know more about. Each chapter begins with a fictional scenario based upon real experiences chairs have faced. After a brief consideration of important concepts, practical tips make up the body of each chapter, followed by questions to be considered privately or more usefully discussed in collegial groups. The chapters in Part I of the book are intended to give readers the orientation they will need as they approach chairing and lead to the first chapter in Part II, "What Chairs Need to Know Their First Day on the Job." The role of the faculty member is discrete and separate from the role of middle managers. How chairs approach their work, the contents of what they do, and what they can expect to accomplish are so different that they require different training and different socialization into role requirements. Chairs need to know from the first day more about the tasks they will have to perform, how much time they need to spend on parts of the job, and the social and emotional requirements of chairing.

The body of the book contains practical advice for department chairs. Many of these tips originated from former and current chairs in response to the question "What best practices have worked for you or your chair colleagues?" Chapters include the following topics:

- Department climate

- Politics

- Budget

- Department meetings

- Time management

- Personnel evaluation and performance counseling

- Challenging personnel

- Legal considerations

- Professional development

- Workload considerations

- How to support teaching and learning

- Chair-dean relations

The book concludes with some thoughts on how to lead, manage, and change the academic department.

How groups go about their work changes with the size of the organization. As colleges grew into small universities, more and more management responsibilities were passed down. As the contemporary college and university has become larger and more complex, oversight and management duties have been increasingly pushed to department-level representatives. While educational philosophy is abstractly debated at the policymaking level, it is increasingly department chairs who have to make education real and concrete. Academic departments, with their tenured faculty, academic senates, and free speech, are particularly good at outlasting change efforts and administrators who come and go at increasingly rapid rates. For change to occur in a timely fashion in higher education institutions, it is largely the department chair who has to make it happen. The department is where most of the action takes place.

For the opportunity to learn the art and craft of management and leadership in academic institutions, I have many to thank. To the leadership and my colleagues at California State University–Chico, I appreciate your confidence as you have allowed me to help steer our course through the stormy seas we have sailed together. To the Office of the Chancellor at the California State University System, I sincerely appreciate the investment you made in my training as Executive Fellow. I never would have learned as much as I know about leadership in the academy if it had not been for the opportunity the CSU System so generously afforded me.

Don Chu
July 2005

Introduction

In the past the man has been first; in the future the system must be first.
—Frederick Taylor, *The Principles of Scientific Management*

Students of higher education in the United States are familiar with the story of the development of today's institutional governance structures. At the turn of the 20th century, faculty in the established and emerging disciplines found it useful to be housed together. Similarities of interest benefited their teaching and scholarship. Central administrators found it both convenient and consistent with the flowcharts of the popular scientific management principles of the period to employ these departments as organizational tools for bureaucratic management. Institutional leaders in America also found it useful to communicate to the faculty through department representatives; a trend that was strengthened as colleges and universities grew in size and diversity. From these groupings, the department emerged as the primary frontline organizational body for the faculty. It is this structure that remains today.

The development of the department and the department chair roughly 100 years ago paralleled an emerging managerial movement in American industry. When Frederick Taylor published *The Principles of Scientific Management* in 1911, it dramatically altered how America went about its work. Taylor recommended that jobs be simplified into discrete pieces that could be easily taught to employees. Perhaps due to his mechanical engineering background, Taylor proposed that by simplifying work, employees could be replaced and the organization would continue to function unimpeded. The autonomy of individual craftsmen was replaced by a formal split between management and employees, and by workers who performed their simple tasks without the need to know more than their own discrete parts in the process. American academic departments followed suit in this organizational pattern. Departments were the place where faculty increasingly became specialists in a scholarly niche, and they were separated from the administration both physically and metaphorically.

Taylor's system of scientific management was the dominant model of organizational management in American industry until the 1960s. Faced with an increasingly competitive worldwide economy, American leaders looked for new ways of working. Following the lead of their Scandinavian and Japanese counterparts, American automakers gave assembly line employees greater rights and responsibilities. Demands for transparency in government following Vietnam and Watergate spread throughout American society. Sunshine laws and the Freedom of Information Act made public officials more responsible for their decisions and actions. Despite all this, however, the social institution at the center of much of the human rights movement remained governed in generally the same way that our colleges and universities had been governed a century before.

Central administration occupies the "management" positions and determines the scope of resources and operational policy to academic units that are directed to produce a certain number of enrollments, majors, graduates, publications, grants, contracts, and the like. In many ways, the management processes of the 21st century remain the same as those employed during the late 19th century. It is little wonder that academic department chairs have been reluctant to assert themselves and lead their institutions. Assignments unidirectionally flow from central administration to the department, where they are either approved and acted upon, merely ignored, or actively resisted by the faculty, who enjoy the protection of tenure that almost guarantees longevity greater than any administrator. But with the increasing size and complexity of departments, dramatic reductions in the levels of public funding of higher education, the subsequent flattening of bureaucracies in search of fiscal efficiency, the necessary growth of interdisciplinary collaborations, and demands for accountability in governance and decision-making, it is increasingly apparent that the role of the department chair requires change. As Ernest Boyer (1990) argued for a new definition of scholarship to include the scholarship of teaching, it is time to include academic leadership within the legitimate expectations of faculty chosen to serve as department leaders.

To chair well requires knowledge of budget, politics, laws and policies, curriculum, human resources, pedagogy, and leadership. While commissions, governors, presidents, provosts, and any number of interest groups may pronounce the need for changes in policies and programs, it is only the chair who most directly impacts changes to who teaches, the courses they teach, the resources they receive to do their work, the recruitment of new faculty, and the conditions under which they grow or wither. While generals direct from high ground, it is the frontline officers and noncommissioned officers who are able to successfully or unsuccessfully translate plans into actions.

Department chairs directly impact the climate in the halls, the perception of the department all across campus, how students and staff are treated, the kind of faculty that want to work there, and the quality of the education that the students receive. There is a scholarship of chairing that draws from the personal talents, intelligence, experience, and wisdom of those elected and chosen to lead the department. Realities of this new age of American higher education demand a new kind of department chair. Rather than serve as the mouthpiece of administration tasked to perform simple acts of department organization, creative, intelligent, wise, experienced, and trained chairs can lead their units; maximize the utilization of scarce resources; take advantage of emerging opportunities; and help faculty to grow as teachers and scholars and in service to their constituents. With so few resources to go around, there is no one more knowledgeable than the chair to distribute resources and match them to the capabilities and interests of the faculty. A chair of a department with 10 full-time faculty typically manages a budget of roughly $1 million. If the chair can better utilize just 1% of that budget, then $10,000 can be used for professional development, student employment or grants, critical equipment, and the like. Seed money invested at the right time can yield great returns upon fruition. Chairs need the same kind of autonomy over their productive processes that assembly line workers received decades ago.

With this responsibility for production, department chairs who are willing to lead also need to accept the responsibility for their actions and decisions. To be able to lead, chairs need training. Since chairing the department is typically an individual's first administrative job, institutions need to make an investment in training university and college leadership. In these pages are practical ideas as to how department chairs can do the best job possible from the first day they move into the main office. What do chairs have to know from the very beginning when they represent the department? Research has shown that the biggest shock to newly minted chairs is the amount of time that bureaucracy requires. I have, therefore, tried to keep this book short. Otherwise, what chair will have the time to read it? The scope of this book is neither theoretical nor grandiose. The intent is to help chairs do as good a job possible from the very first day.

Most everyone working in higher education is there for the same purpose—to serve society by advancing knowledge to those capable of understanding and using it for the benefit of others. As resources diminish while social needs grow, it is increasingly important that chairs serve their academic units by maximizing the good work of their departments. For faculty to do their best work, talents need to be matched with resources and the opportunity to serve. Due to the chair's personal knowledge of the talents of the faculty, oversight of the resources of the department, and understanding of department and institutional directions, the chair is uniquely positioned to promote good works for the benefit of faculty careers, student welfare, and social improvement. It is both a privilege and a responsibility to do so.

PART I

WHAT CHAIRS NEED TO KNOW TO UNDERSTAND THEIR DEPARTMENTS AND THEIR NEW ROLES

Departments and Colleges as Open and Closed Systems

Before becoming chairs, faculty were taught theoretical bases that were critical to understand the issues they would have to face as professors in their disciplines. The need for some theoretical perspective also holds true for faculty who become department chairs. What do chairs need to know about their roles? It is useful to see academic departments as formal organizations.

Formal organizations have explicit goals, specified productive processes to achieve those goals, official roles, clear statuses, rights, and duties. Sociological formal organizational theory illustrates the complexity of the department chair role as members of formal organizations called departments, colleges, and universities.

Formal Organizations as Open and Closed Systems

Faculty tend to see their departments as closed systems, whereby that which is most important occurs within the organization (see Figure 1.1).

Figure 1.1
Departments as Closed Systems

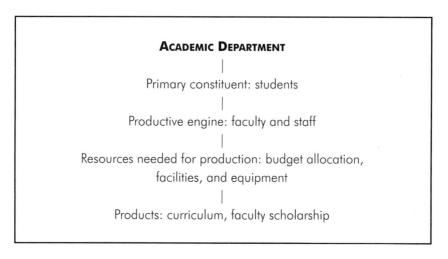

ACADEMIC DEPARTMENT
|
Primary constituent: students
|
Productive engine: faculty and staff
|
Resources needed for production: budget allocation,
facilities, and equipment
|
Products: curriculum, faculty scholarship

In this view of academic departments as closed systems, the primary work of the organization goes on within its classrooms, labs, and offices. The faculty, staff, and administration employ budget, facilities, and equipment to serve the only client group that matters—the students. Since chairs come from the faculty, and most of their previous experience has been centered on their individual teaching and scholarship, it is not unusual for new chairs to assume that their departments are central to the institution. In fact, not every subunit of the college and university can be central to the mission, culture, and future of the larger organization. It is more useful to employ an open systems perspective than a closed systems perspective when chairs think about their departments (see Figure 1.2).

If departments are viewed in this fashion, department chairs are boundary spanners who work between the formal organization and each of the constituent groups surrounding the organization. Boundary spanners work both within the unit and outside the department. In this picture of how academic departments operate, it is both good internal work and work with external groups that will determine the success enjoyed by the unit. If the department is to be best resourced with students, allocations, contributions, prestige, community and alumni support, and the like, then how well the chair works with faculty, staff, and students within the department, and with each of the external groups important to the department, will determine the department's success.

Figure 1.2
Departments as Open Systems

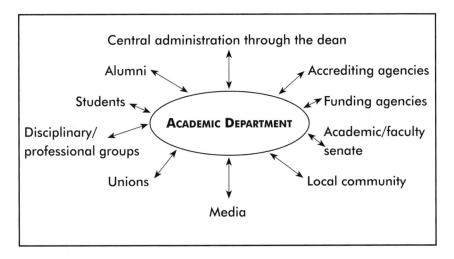

In the open system, the formal organization is viewed as embedded within and dependent upon the external environment for the resources the department needs to do its work. In return for course credits, for instance, learners provide themselves as the primary resource needed by the department to do its work; that is, they provide themselves as students. The central administration provides budget allocations in return for the kind of programs and faculty accomplishments deemed by deans, vice presidents, and presidents to be in the best interests of the institution. In return for a curriculum that resembles association requirements, legitimizing agencies provide accreditation. In return for the pride that a quality program can provide, alumni provide contributions. In return for scholarship from the faculty, their disciplines provide prestige. In return for services, funding agencies provide grants and contract dollars, and so on and so on.

In the closed systems perspective, it is assumed that the central work of the organization is internal and that most of what matters to the health and welfare of that organization's members is what they do within their units. Contemporary colleges and universities should also be seen as open systems, because how each subunit relates to outside constituencies will have a direct effect on that unit. For the academic department, its internal work—teaching, advising, and curricular programming—is obviously important, but what is also important is the faculty scholarship, campus committee work, alumni relations, academic senate memberships, and other activities that relate the department to constituents in the environment who hold the resources and support the department needs to do its work most effectively. How the department is perceived in the larger context of other departments, other campus offices, in the scholarly field, and in the community has a bearing on the power of the department to do its work well. It is the department chair's responsibility to understand both internal and external constituencies and to work with those elements of the environment important to the work of the department. Each important constituent group wants certain product outcomes from the department, and in return, that constituent group holds resources that the department may benefit from. It is important for chairs to understand the dynamics of this exchange, to determine what each constituent group wants from the department, and to maximize the resource flow into the department from each of the constituent groups without jeopardizing the status of the unit or violating the mission of the department. Resources important to the department may include money, support for some program from influential alumni or board members, positive public relations, excellent entering students, accolades, and scholarship donations. Support from outside constituencies can mean the difference between a department that is constantly scrutinized and criticized or a department that is always assumed to be doing a great job. It can mean the difference between a department that is threatened during lean budget years and a department that is looked to as so exemplary that it is perceived to be central to the mission and future of the university.

2

UNDERSTANDING THE INSTITUTION AND ITS PROCESSES

*Professor Knight and Professor Day were elected chairs of their depart-
ments last May, but Professor Day has a much better idea of how to
approach her job than does Professor Knight. Chair Day knows the
important policies, people, and programs to guide, while Chair Knight
is in the dark, learning on the job. In their college meetings with the
dean, Chair Day is on top of things. It's obvious from her comments that
she is familiar with local campus politics, changes in policies and new
funding opportunities. Chair Knight, on the other hand, needs to learn
more about a particular issue, and he is behind when it comes to important campus information. It's now April and both have been tasked to
make new position proposals to their dean. Chair Knight worries if he
will do an adequate job, especially in light of the persuasive arguments
always forwarded by Chair Day. Chair Knight knows how to attack
research questions in his discipline, but he wonders how he can better
understand the dynamics of his role as chair in very short order.*

If American higher education is viewed as an open system whose welfare
and ability to accomplish its objectives is dependent upon both those within
the institution and those outside of it, what should chairs know? Even more

elementary, how should they go about determining what they need to know? Just as faculty have been taught a body of knowledge and methodologies appropriate for their disciplines, academic leaders also have a body of information they will need to know to do their work.

MAKING SENSE OF ORGANIZATIONS

As biologists, sociologists, and historians have learned how to analyze problems to better understand them and then plan the most appropriate research methods to employ, higher education managers and leaders need to learn how to understand the bureaucracies in which they work. While the modest size of families and small businesses may call for informal interactions to communicate what is necessary to guide the small group, the large size of colleges and universities requires a different approach. To understand organizations, and then to plan appropriate courses of action, chairs, deans, and central administrators can benefit from looking at their units through a number of organizational frames of reference.

According to Bolman and Deal (1997), organizations can be viewed through the following lenses:

- *Structural frame:* Official groups, positions, and policies to govern their relationships

- *Human resources frame:* Human needs within the organization

- *Political frame:* Power, conflict, and coalitions

- *Symbolic frame:* Organizational culture and symbols, organizations as theater

The *structural frame* refers to the official and public rules and offices in the bureaucracy that regulate organizational behavior. These rules provide the parameters within which the department and its leaders are expected to operate. In the administrative flowchart, what are the groups, positions, and polices of most importance to the department? Is it the students, alumni, faculty, faculty associations, accrediting bodies, senior full professors, or other official offices? What do official documents say these offices can and cannot do? Are there certain policy directives, contractual terms, laws, bylaws, or other official documents that prevent the department from being all that it is capable of becoming?

The *human resources frame* will help chairs understand the department and its environment. Who are the most important members of the organization who impact the effectiveness of the unit? Faculty, students, staff, and administrators both inside and outside of the department all have their personal goals, motivations, and agendas. What drives these people who are most essential to the effectiveness of the department? Chairs who understand the most important needs and desires of those with whom they work will have an important insight into the criteria that are employed to determine the actions of those so important to department operations.

The *political frame* assumes that issues important to the department will have various constituent groups lining up to support or oppose the position most favorable to the department. Chairs need to determine who is aligned with whom on what issues. Although birds of a feather flock together, it is also true that politics makes strange bedfellows. Chairs who understand the political positions of those with whom they deal can tailor their actions and messages to best position their departments.

Lastly, the *symbolic frame* needs to be considered. Chairs need to know where the line in the sand is. Is it a particular course that represents the historical, sacred work of a faculty member and cannot be removed from the schedule? If a chair is working with an alumni group, is it free access to the department's events that means so much that there can never be an attendance charge? Is it a certain class size that cannot be broached without a major confrontation with the senior faculty? Most anything can become a symbol, whether it is a mascot, a piece of cloth that becomes an institutional flag, or the football team that represents the perceived identity of the school.

Academic departments operate within a bureaucratic context that needs to be understood by chairs. As they help their units negotiate with allies and opponents, groups within the college and university will seek to achieve their own objectives. Bolman and Deal's model will help chairs make sense of the bureaucracy and the internal and external constituent groups that will affect the department's performance.

3

WHEN A FACULTY MEMBER BECOMES A DEPARTMENT CHAIR

Along with his promotion to full professor and a large salary increase due to his new, highly acclaimed book, Dr. Sy Nigh also became the new department chair. During his first days in the big office, however, Dr. Nigh was surprised to find out just how different being a chair was from being a faculty member. The historical research that gained him professional accolades and promotion seemed far removed from the whirlwind of meetings about other people's problems, follow-through on plans made well before his tenure, and the crises that forced their way into his daily schedule. Dr. Nigh was determined to serve his department faculty and students, and to do everything he could to transform the curriculum and acquire needed instructional equipment. But he is already being blamed for problems that he didn't create. His friends seem to treat him differently. He finds that he cannot share confidential information, even with his family. He wonders if his allegiances are with his friends, or the department, or the university. His children are also about to start college, and he knows that previous salary increases were due to scholarly productivity. He wonders if his salary will stagnate for three years if he tries his best to help his department and the faculty to be more productive.

The last two chairs in the Department of English held the job on an acting basis. They saw themselves as caretakers until someone else was elected who was willing to put service to the department before their own work. Professor Rush is just the person for the job. As motivated as she is to serve her colleagues, however, she finds herself unexpectedly unprepared for the first day of work. This is her first administrative position as she has followed the typical career path of most new chairs. She earned her Ph.D. and then tenure based upon her scholarship and teaching. Now she knows that administration is a brand new role. She hasn't received training through workshops or mentoring programs. It's tough enough getting in touch with anyone during the summer term before she becomes chair. All she's gotten to inform her about what she'll have to do is a "job description" for chairs that resembles a laundry list of everything she'll be responsible for, but she wants to know what's most important. What can she be expected to do on a daily basis? She has resigned herself to the knowledge that she will have to learn on the job, but she doesn't know what she'll really be spending her time doing, what she'll really have to know, what she'll need to focus on. Furthermore, department funding in her college is competitive and based on data-driven budget presentations. She's been warned that Dr. Bight and the Department of Marketing have received substantial budget increases recently, purportedly at the expense of other departments in her college that were not as well prepared in their budget request proposals. She wonders if she'll do justice to her department.

Anyone who has been an academic chair knows that the role of faculty member is markedly different from their new role of department chair. What happens to that person once they move to the department office?

CHANGING ROLES: FROM FACULTY MEMBER TO DEPARTMENT CHAIR

It is a sociological principle that individuals stand distinct from the roles that they fill. Especially in larger departments, it is a managerial fact that bureaucracy inevitably rears its head in the main office, relations and expectations change, and behavior varies from what we were accustomed to when we had coffee together as professors.

Very few faculty are formally prepared for the role of department chair. From the very first day, new chairs find that the disciplinary and scholarly skills that were the primary criteria for career success as faculty members have little to do with the new requirements of managing and leading academic departments. The sociological concept of *role* is useful in understanding what happens to faculty once they accept this new chair's position. With the role of chair comes a new set of behavioral expectations, attitudinal sets, and objectives. This transformation is illustrated in Figure 3.1.

Figure 3.1
The Transformation From Professor to Chair

PROFESSOR	CHAIR
Solitary	Social
Manuscripts	Memos
Stability	Mobility
Austerity	Prosperity
Client	Custodian
Professing	Persuading
Autonomy	Accountability
Focused	Fragmented

Note. Adapted from Gmelch (2000).

Solitary to Social

Faculty typically have six to twelve hours of classes and office hours per week to account for. The rest of the working day can be divided up as they see fit.

13

Chairs need to be publicly available most hours of most days to meet with students, faculty, staff, and administrators, even when it is inconvenient to their professional and personal schedules. The alumni, community, and professional constituents need to be able to communicate with the department through the chair, and chairs need to represent the department at meetings, socials, and other events.

Manuscripts to Memos

Manuscripts require the uninterrupted time that faculty have available. Department chairs typically don't have the luxury of spans of time. They have to write memos instead, and short briefing papers that will be read by similarly harried administrators. Chairs need to be able to digest a great deal of information and then summarize concisely positions and options, eventually laying out the best course of action in their professional opinion. Uninterrupted time is typically only available to department chairs in the early hours of the morning while the rest of the world is fast asleep.

Stability to Mobility

The security and longevity brought to faculty by tenure renders them as occupationally stable as the justices on the Supreme Court. Once the faculty member elected to the position of chair assumes that role, however, it is by definition an impermanent one. And chairs deal with other administrators who are also in impermanent positions. Administrators move up, or down, or sideways. Administration is a mobile business.

Austerity to Prosperity

Faculty are usually accustomed to making do. Unless they have their own operating account, there are typically many more calls on the money available to the department than there is money to go around. Department chairs often have access to monetary accounts unavailable to the faculty. Foundation or grant-funded accounts, operating monies set aside for equipment purchase and maintenance, money for salaries of temporary faculty, new money unallocated the previous year, and money rolled over from previous years is available to the chair for distribution with the chair's approval.

Client to Custodian

Faculty are clients in many senses of the term. They benefit from the services of the accounting office, benefits personnel, campus security, the copy shop, and food services. Chairs are custodians in the sense that it is their responsibility to see to it that faculty are served appropriately by all campus offices and officers. The chair is the custodian of the rights of the faculty and staff in the department.

Professing to Persuading

A faculty member's primary responsibility is to profess; that is, to publicly declare his or her version of truth so as to educate students and advance learning. The chair's position requires a much greater level of wariness. As the representative of the department, chairs are not nearly as free to express their own opinions. They must take into account the diversity of opinion in their departments, the perceptions of those with whom they communicate, and the possible repercussions of any public proclamation on behalf of the department. Because chairs have a fiduciary responsibility, they must exercise caution. The position of chair is limited in power, and any exercise of power reduces the political capital available in the future. Chairs exercise influence through persuasion much more than through power.

Autonomy to Accountability

Faculty are autonomous in the sense that they do not typically have to answer for their work. Classes are taught behind closed doors, papers are presented away from campus, and publications are refereed before they become public.

When a department chair makes a decision, spends funds, schedules classes, and writes a faculty evaluation, however, the public nature of that work immediately requires the chair to be accountable to some public.

Focused to Fragmented

Faculty are able to focus their thoughts and energies to a much greater extent than can department chairs. Faculty can more easily prepare for their days because their schedules are more predictable than the chair's. Students, faculty, and staff stop into the chair's office with something of immediate importance to them. Memos and reports have to be researched and written on short or no notice. Some pleasant event such as an awards ceremony can be immediately followed by some much less happy event such as a negative evaluation or disciplinary procedure. Chairing can be an emotional roller coaster.

EXPECTATIONS AND SURPRISES FOR NEW CHAIRS

Department chairs are expected to administer department operations and lead the organization into the future. Most new chairs do not have sufficient training and/or experience to fully understand their new roles. Research conducted on 425 chairs from a 23-campus system has shown that few faculty are formally prepared for their new roles as department chairs (Chu & Veregge, 2002). Chairs were asked the question "How does the position of chair differ from the expectations you held for the position before you became chair?" Table 3.1 shows the percentage of chairs who indicated "less than expected" and "more than expected."

Respondents were clearly most surprised by the time and paperwork required for the role. The routing requirements of paperwork and meetings left less time than expected for the kind of creative work and projects that might forward the department or the faculty and that professors normally engage in as part of their faculty roles.

Table 3.1
How Chairing Differs From Expectations

How Chairing Differs From Expectations	Less Than Expected	More Than Expected
The amount of time the job takes	1%	79%
The amount of paperwork	1%	79%
The number of meetings	4%	45%
The strain that being chair puts on my relationship with faculty	17%	35%
The support I receive from my dean	26%	25%
The support I expect from the faculty	23%	37%
Opportunities to make a positive impact	23%	26%
How rewarding the job is	34%	28%
The support I receive from central administration	45%	11%
The amount of time after the routine work is done to undertake projects or creative activities	78%	21%

WHAT DO CHAIRS DO WITH THEIR TIME?

Now that we have seen what chairs expected, and what they were surprised to find, it is useful to see what research has found regarding the tasks that chairs must perform. Specifically, what do chairs do during their workdays? Table 3.2 shows chairs' responses to the question, "Indicate how much of your time as chair is consumed by each of the activities listed below."

Table 3.2
What Do Chairs Have to Do?

RANK	TASKS	GREAT DEAL OF TIME	LITTLE TIME
1	Reading/responding to memos from other offices	55%	5%
2	Writing reports	50%	10%
3	Reading administratively relevant material	38%	11%
3	Staffing classes	38%	19%
4	Scheduling classes and rooms	37%	21%
4	Recruiting staff and faculty	37%	18%
5	Budget management and planning	34%	19%
6	Managing staff and faculty	33%	21%
6	Advising students/ student complaints	33%	9%

Rank	Tasks	Great Deal of Time	Little Time
6	Program planning/ curriculum development	33%	14%
7	Representing department at college- or university-level meetings	32%	16%
8	Leading or attending department meetings	30%	11%
9	Doing program assessment	26%	21%
9	Teaching	26%	19%
10	Review, tenure, and promotion	23%	12%
11	Creating course/program assessment plans	21%	38%
12	Faculty and staff evaluations	18%	24%
12	Faculty and staff personnel problems	18%	38%
13	Scholarly activity	13%	45%
14	Establishing partnerships with off-campus entities	12%	51%
15	Public relations	11%	43%
16	Faculty and staff development	9%	50%

Rank	Tasks	Great Deal of Time	Little Time
17	Fundraising	8%	68%
18	Management space	7%	52%
19	Requesting/negotiating repairs to rooms/buildings	6%	71%
20	Managing large equipment repair/ replacement	5%	71%
21	Planning and negotiating remodeling	4%	73%
21	Writing grants	4%	69%

Source. Chu and Veregge (2002).

The most time-consuming tasks for department chairs can be characterized as *bureaucratic grind*. This is the kind of work that is unfamiliar to new administrators and therefore takes more time than might otherwise be expended by more seasoned administrators. These tasks involve the writing and reading required for responding and reporting (note these are the first three tasks indicated in Table 3.2). Chairs must respond to emails, letters, calls, and appointment requests. Much of this is time-sensitive and needs to happen quickly. Reading background material, policy documents, and technical interpretations takes a great deal of time for chairs who typically do not have the administrative support staff to do the trench work otherwise done by deans', vice presidents', and presidents' staffs. It will take new chairs time to learn how to efficiently handle all the tasks required of them in the department office.

The next set of tasks (#3–#6) may be referred to as the *household routine*. The head of household needs to ensure that all of the chores have someone assigned to them. He or she has to listen to everyone's problems and deal with complaints. The head of household tries to establish consensus (if possible) about what the organization actually does as it tries to reach its goals. This is the kind of daily work that has to be done or the organization cannot function efficiently.

QUESTIONS TO CONSIDER

1) How well does Gmelch's model (depicted in Figure 3.1) fit the department chairs on your campus? Explain your response.

2) Does becoming department chair hurt or help the chair's scholarly work?

3) Does the reward system on your campus fit the role of faculty better than department chairs?

4) Apply the Gmelch model to yourself. How applicable are these changes to you?

5) Do you expect that your personal life will be affected by the role demands of chairing? If yes, in what ways?

6) After you complete your term as chair, how do expect that your outlook on departmental and institutional governance will change?

7) How much would you agree with the following statements?
   (1 = strongly disagree; 5 = strongly agree)

   ____ Acting as chair has strained my relations with the faculty in my department.

   ____ I receive little support from my dean.

   ____ I receive little support from central administration.

   ____ I have little opportunity to make a positive impact on my faculty.

   ____ I have little time after routine work to undertake creative projects.

8) Plot out a typical first week of the academic term. Assuming a hypothetical 40-hour work week, how many hours might be allocated to meetings, reading and writing reports, teaching, managing budgets, managing rooms/scheduling/equipment, human resources issues, student complaints and advising, personal scholarship, and other matters?

9) List the groups and individuals with whom you regularly meet. How often should you expect to meet with each group and individual?

10) List the reports you will have to read regularly.

11) List the reports you will have to produce regularly.

12) With whom will you communicate regularly? For what purpose(s)?

Part II

What Chairs Need to Know to Do Their Jobs

4

WHAT CHAIRS NEED TO KNOW THEIR FIRST DAY ON THE JOB

*Professor Sharp is a newly appointed chair. Despite his academic exper-
tise in organizational management, he only has the boilerplate job
description for his campus's chairs to give him any idea of what he is
about to face. The job description is just an encyclopedic list of everything that chairs may be responsible for, regardless of the discipline, the
college, if it is or is not an accreditation year, and the particulars of economic or political circumstances. Professor Sharp has been around long
enough to know that this list cannot tell him what his priorities should
be, how to position himself and his department, and generally how to
accomplish all of the tasks listed on the job description. Today is his first
day in the department office. He wonders what he is going to really
have to do. He knows that new organizational roles require the appropriate attitude and emotional dispositions, and there is nothing in the
job description about this. Nor is there anything about who to ask for
answers to particular questions, who to trust, and what to do with the
strategic plan, if anything. The chair's desk is completely covered with
paperwork and there is a backlog of emails. He has to figure out what
he should do quickly or he fears that he'll never get ahead and always be
playing catch-up.*

This is a typical scenario that faces department chairs their first day on the job. With little formal socialization into their new management and leadership role, faculty who become academic leaders face an unknown behind the department chair's door. Job descriptions usually list what chairs will be responsible for. They do not tell chairs what they need to know to perform effectively in their new role. A job description that lists responsibilities does little to prepare chairs. Role performance requires expertise in the execution of discrete tasks, but it also requires certain attitudes and dispositions that affect how the role of chair is approached.

Based upon the advice of experienced chairs, what does a newly appointed department chair need to know from the very first day?

1) *Chairs officially represent the department.* Be cognizant of what you say, how you say it, and what you do, and be sensitive to the interpretations of those with whom you interact as representative of your department.

2) *Chairs are the primary department officers charged with protecting the rights of faculty and staff and ensuring that they fulfill their legal and ethical responsibilities.* These rights and responsibilities are contained in department and institutional policies, the American Association of University Professors Code of Ethics, state and community laws, and the U.S. Constitution.

3) *Chairs are members of the team that is leading the institution as well as their own academic unit.* Before acting, sympathize with the administrators with whom you are working to understand their legitimate points of view.

4) *Chairs are usually not personally liable for actions undertaken in the course of fulfilling their professional responsibilities, but there are exceptions.* The exceptions include actions taken outside the scope of the chair's job description, or action that is unprofessional, malicious, reckless, or imprudent.

5) *Maintain confidentiality.* New chairs suddenly have access to a great deal of personal information about those in the department.

6) *The best sources of information on how to be a good chair are the best chairs on campus.* Find out who they are and develop good communications with them.

7) *How much chairs are able to do is largely dependent upon how much support their deans are willing and able to publicly provide.* Cultivate your relationship with the dean. Meet with the dean individually and regularly, as well as in public settings.

8) *Credibility is the chair's most important personal asset.* Mean what you say, and do what you say you will do. Never be afraid to say "I made a mistake" or "I am sorry."

9) *Who you spend time with should have your undivided attention.* Because the chair's schedule is so busy, there is always the temptation to look ahead or behind. Resist this impulse; the people you are with have business to attend to that is very important to them.

10) *Maximize the talents of the faculty.* Help faculty connect their talents to what the institution is trying to do for students.

11) *Chairs have a fiduciary responsibility* to see to it that all resources (money, curriculum, facilities and equipment, personnel) are fully utilized and safeguarded for the future.

12) *Chairs should operationalize the strategic plan into achievable pieces and make daily decisions in support of the plan.* Chairs should be able to justify every decision according to how it moves the department toward realization of its strategic plan.

13) *Not every problem is a real problem.* Many problems are really opportunities in disguise. Chairs who creatively look for means to reframe obstacles into opportunities have a leg up on nay-sayers who regularly see the sky falling.

14) *There are two types of chairs: reactive chairs and proactive chairs.* Reactive chairs range from do-nothing or do-little-at-all chairs to excellent managers who fulfill their supervisory responsibilities. Proactive chairs are good enough managers that their departments fulfill their obligations within the organization's budget and programmatic constraints,

and they are motivated to take the steps to improve their department's services to students, faculty, and staff. Chairs of this type go out of their way to provide the environment and direction to maximize the talents of the faculty toward the achievement of greater institutional goals.

15) *Chairs can make a real difference* in how much the faculty develop and grow professionally, the quality of the curriculum that students receive and how well it prepares them for their futures, how well the department serves the community and society, and how well the department is positioned for future growth or reduction.

QUESTIONS TO CONSIDER

1) Choose the top three items from the list above that you believe are most useful for chairs to know the first day they are on the job. Explain your response.

2) Who are the best chairs on your campus? Explain your response.

3) How much do you think chairs on your campus operationalize their strategic plans? Explain your response.

4) How important do you believe item #10 (maximize the talents of the faculty) to be? Why have you responded as you have?

5

DEPARTMENT CLIMATE

On this unionized campus, all departments operate within the same contract, yet there is a markedly different feel about the Department of Geosciences compared with the Department of Biology. Professor Shirley Kuhl has been chair of the Department of Geosciences for several years. She has put a great deal of effort into making the department resemble the geosciences department where she earned her doctorate. Faculty chatted in the halls, they collaborated on grants, they also team taught and covered for each other when one of their colleagues was away from campus fulfilling professional responsibilities. This enthusiasm for their work is obvious in the halls, in the classroom, and in the field when students and faculty go away for extended field experiences. In the biology department, however, department chair Tom Ult faces a very different environment. He is the third chair in as many years that has had to deal with a poisonous department climate. People just don't want to come to work in the biology building. The faculty are divided into warring camps based upon decades-old slights and disrespect. There is little collaboration, and faculty don't visit with each other or hang around much after their office hours. Students sense this animosity based on comments faculty make about each other in class. Around campus, leaders in the senate and administration have had to get involved in the intradepart-

*ment bickering, and communications flow is based less upon who needs
to know and more upon who knows and likes whom. Department personnel problems have become increasingly public in the campus paper.
As faculty have retired, recruitment of replacements has been problematic since the lack of collegiality is easy to sense. What new faculty would
want to walk into a combat zone? As a result, the biology department
is in decline, with faculty positions being shifted to other departments,
reduced operating budgets, and little hope for a better future.*

This scenario is not uncommon. On most campuses there exists a range
of department climates. Faced with the same demographics and contract,
departments can have very different environments ranging from enthusiastic, collaborative, and intellectually exciting to deadening, isolated, and
depressing.

For the academy to function best, there should be an atmosphere of trust,
respect, and collegiality. Ideas are the coin of the realm in the academy, and
ideas are most freely exchanged when faculty and staff value each other and
respect each other's opinions. In the best departments, the climate is one that
invites expression, exploration and inquiry. If there is one area that chairs
most directly impact, it is their department's climate. What do chairs need
to bear in mind relative to the environment in their department halls and
offices?

1) *Department climate is the chair's responsibility.* Because chairs command
   the department agenda, are its most public figure internally, represent the
   department externally, and must sign off on expenditures and schedules,
   chairs can either make the department the kind of place conducive to
   productive, fulfilling labor, or a place where no one wants to spend much
   time.

2) *Chairs can have a positive effect on the department environment by model-
   ing the characteristics they wish their faculty, staff, and students to exhibit.*
   Chairs are not only positional leaders, but they are, just as importantly,
   symbolic leaders of the department. If chairs want their faculty to respect
   others and value intellectual excitement, chairs need to exhibit these
   qualities in their daily interactions.

3) *The chair position is a service position.* By serving the faculty, chairs help make them feel important and valued. Chairs serve the faculty so that the faculty can serve their students, the institution, their disciplines, and their community. The engine that drives the institution is the faculty, and that engine deserves the support of administration.

4) *Chairs need to be knowledgeable and competent.* In the academy, knowledge is most closely linked to competence. Chairs who don't know what they are doing, who don't know how to efficiently translate intent into action, who don't have the information important for department affairs, who miss deadlines, who don't know who to ask or how to get the information critical to department affairs, will quickly poison the department's atmosphere.

5) *The chair's work should be as transparent as possible.* With the exception of privileged personnel matters, issues of budget, schedule, planning, and communications coming into and going outside of the department need to be publicly and easily available. Secrecy is the most certain means of fouling the air in the department's corridors.

6) *Chairs should see themselves as equal.* They need to see themselves as no better or worse than any other faculty member. This makes sense if we accept that the primary coin of the college realm is ideas. Ideas are not limited to senior faculty, tenured faculty, or administration. The best ideas come from the most talented, the best educated, and the most well trained. Chairs who can convey that they are equal to the faculty will gain the trust and respect of their colleagues far more easily than an imperial chair.

7) *Chairs must be objective.* Chairs should not allow their personal biases and interpretations to take over the department. Pet programs that are disproportionately funded, allies unjustifiably appointed to influential posts, debates decided without appropriate discourse and consideration are all means by which the climate of the department can putrefy. Chairs need to listen, respect interpretations and perceptions that may run counter to their own, carefully weigh significant points on all sides of an issue, and then publicly convey the reasons why a decision has been reached. Chairs cannot insulate themselves from criticism, but they can

31

guard against criticism that decisions have not been made as objectively as possible.

8) *Chairs must be credible.* What chairs say, what they promise, their explanations, and even their apologies must be believable. Chairs must be credible as well as consistent in what they say. To change the story dependent on the audience is too political and only leads to more and more office politics.

9) *Chairs must respect all members of the department.* Too often department leadership favors those with a point of view similar to its own. Respect needs to be given to faculty both junior and senior, those productive and those less so, to the staff, student workers, and all students. As the most public member of the department, the chair must model respect, which is a necessity for free department discourse. The chair shows respect for members of the department by recognizing that they are individuals, each with his or her own story, history, and culture. For example, recognition of important days and events in their lives shows faculty and staff that they are respected as people as well as employees.

10) *Chairs must be humble.* As the world changes and knowledge exponentially multiplies, humility may be the only reliable truth. Boastful chairs that claim department achievements as their own destroy the department climate.

11) *Department climate is bolstered by demonstrations of appreciation for jobs well done.* Public kudos during department meetings, awards for superior teaching, scholarship, or service, and any public recognition in campus or department newspapers or web sites makes department personnel feel appreciated. When we feel appreciated, we happily return to places where we have been appreciated.

12) *Chairs need to protect the confidentiality of the privileged information they receive.* Although it may be habit to discuss interesting new information, any revelation of otherwise confidential information will quickly destroy the often hard-won confidence that the chair has earned from department colleagues. Even more important, it is unethical to treat someone's personal information with anything other than the greatest respect.

QUESTIONS TO CONSIDER

1) Choose two departments on your campus with different climates. Describe the climates in each department. Why are they different? What can the chairs of each department do to improve their departments' climates?

2) What can chairs do to build their credibility? What can chairs do to destroy their credibility?

3) How can department chairs show that they respect their colleagues?

6

POLITICS

Professor Evelyn Ready has been chair of the Department of Nursing for seven years. She and her department are well positioned on campus. They have faculty in key senate and administrative positions, a very active alumni association, and their advisory board is a who's who of the city's medical, business, and political community. Almost every year the nursing department lands a major grant or contract that enlarges its contact pool in the community, and that increases the discretionary budget for professional development. Despite ongoing campus budget reductions, the nursing department does not seem to be negatively affected. If anything, it may actually benefit from the consolidation of the Department of Health Services and the Department of Nursing, transforming them into the School of Nursing and Health Services, with Professor Ready as the director of the school. Before coming to campus, Dr. Ready managed forward operations for the Army. There and on campus, she learned to have information available before it was immediately needed and reports pre-drafted. She learned how to prepare presentations to convince constituents and win friends. She always seems to be able to anticipate what is over the horizon, and be prepared to take advantage of opportunities.

On every campus there are a few chairs like Evelyn Ready who are able to advance their departments while others are at risk for damage. How do these department leaders position their units? While evidence, discussion, and reason are ideally the means through which campuses make decisions, anyone with experience on a college campus knows how much political maneuvering goes on. It is incumbent, then, that chairs be politically adept so that they can best serve their departments.

Politics is most generally defined as social relations involving authority or power. Given the contemporary economic fact that there never seem to be enough resources to go around, allocation decisions need to be made. Decisions that occur in public venues, such as on campuses, invariably require political calculation. The fact that the department chair operates at a middle level of management requires that chairs look at the dynamics of the social relations of faculty, staff, and students in the department and the college and greater campus in which the department is embedded.

The bureaucratic structures that dominate campus organizations today invariably lead to differences in authority and power. Difference in authority and power between organizational members is a fact of higher education administration in the United States. Although the use of raw power to make administrative decisions in colleges is frowned upon, it is not entirely absent. Chairs need to recognize that their positions at the legal head of the department make them, by definition, holders of greater power and authority than their peers. Although faculty may be skeptical about power, the more relevant question for academic leaders is how can chairs employ political power to benefit the good work of the department. What do they need to know and do so that the faculty will have what they need to do their best work?

1) *Politics stems from social relations.* Those holding roles in the social structure of the organization interact. A key to political success is to understand the motivations of those with whom you interact. If chairs can understand where organizational members are coming from, where they want to go, and why they want to go there, it helps chairs to place their department's agenda in context and to know how to act with those influencing the organization's decisions.

2) *Political problems require time to resolve.* Politics is not finite mathematics. Politics involves people, their feelings, and their intellect. Campus political issues are best resolved for the long run when there is a felt sense of general agreement. Don't rush to a quick solution that may make sense rationally until major players feel comfortable and confident about the resolution.

3) *Politically savvy chairs conduct environmental scans no less than once per year.* Look for continuity and change in opportunities and dangers to the department. Try to see over the horizon so that you can position your department to get ahead of difficulties before they become problems and so that your department can take advantage of opportunities before everyone else gets in line.

4) *Visualize a flowchart of administrative positions on campus to see which offices are the locus among other positions in the organization.* Metaphorically, the shortstop is involved in more communication and action in that organization than is the left fielder. Get to know those on campus at the center of most of the action. Get to know those with the information that your department will need. These people include deans, vice presidents, admissions, plant operations, external grant officers, institutional research, and the alumni office.

5) *Chairs must get to know their staff.* While office directors may have authority and official power, staff members often come into greater contact with other campus members and their communications. If you allow staff members to know what your department's needs are, if they believe that chairs have legitimate and reasonable needs for information, staff can facilitate the communication of that information. It is usually a great deal easier to contact staff members than it is to contact office directors who are in meetings most of the day.

6) *Chairs can understand political dynamics better if they analyze coalitional blocks.* This means who is allied with whom and on what issue. Part of the chair's role, then, is to develop like-minded coalitions so that they may influence policy and practice to their mutual benefit. The coalitional members of importance will vary with the issue. On some issues, coalitional members may include campus leaders such as chairs, deans,

senators, vice presidents, the president, and their staff. On other issues, coalition members may be enlisted from off campus including alumni, community leaders, and political and opinion leaders.

7) *Campus politics is usually civil and rarely of the bare-knuckle brawl variety.* Campus politics typically resembles the U.S. Senate, where long-term incumbents engage in civilized debate, vote, and then move on to the next issue. The fact that all parties know they will have to live together for a long time tends to moderate emotion.

8) *Power should only be used as a last resort.* Only resort to power after reason and exchange have been tried to settle differences between members of the group. It is a political maxim that the use of power renders the user less powerful in the future.

9) *Allies are much easier to work with than enemies.* The best political outcome is when disputes are resolved and all parties perceive that they have won. The existence of tenure means that chairs will have to work with the same people for a very long time.

10) *A political victory achieved at the expense of an opponent who has been publicly embarrassed can become a long-term loss.* Losing on an issue is one thing. Losing face or reputation is much more damaging.

11) *Politically speaking, it is almost impossible for a chair to fight and win against a dean or other central administrator.* Since most chairs serve at the pleasure of the dean, provost, or president, any chair willing to publicly fight against a central administrator had better be ready to step down or be fired.

12) *Every political issue is only important to the extent that it relates to the individual and his or her position.* Get to know the personal perspective of everyone in the institution that is an important officer, faculty, and staff member who may have some influence over what happens to your unit.

13) *Remember that politics cannot be personal.* Representatives of various campus units need to act in the best interests of the college and university as they see best interests defined from their perspectives. Chairs should not take personally the actions of campus officers that are inconsistent with the best interests of their departments.

14) *The chair's first responsibility is to take care of home.* For most new chairs, this role is their first opportunity to access administrative offices, the public external to their departments, and opportunities for leadership in administration. This novelty can be very exciting, but chairs need to remember to first put their best efforts into maintaining and improving the delivery of services to their department's faculty, staff, and students. To do otherwise would be to take advantage of the trust that the department has given the chair to manage its affairs in the best interests of the faculty, staff, and students. With careful time management, experienced chairs should then have sufficient time and energy for service to other constituencies beyond their departments. But chairs must never neglect home.

15) *Credibility is a chair's most important political asset.* Those with whom chairs interact need to know that what chairs say is accurate, that they will do what they say they will do, and that there is no personal or selfish intent motivating the chair.

16) *Political capital is another important asset.* Political capital results from jobs particularly well done and from useful information that is provided. It can result from a timely personal introduction to some campus official or from some gesture that shows unexpected generosity or compassion. Those who develop a reputation for being knowledgeable, unselfish, credible, and effective have much more political capital than those who are ineffective, self-promoting blowhards.

17) *Political power can result from a superior officer who authorizes an action, but it can also come from an officer who does not prohibit an action.* In other words, by not issuing an order prohibiting some action, a superior officer may provide a chair with the political room to maneuver on behalf of the department.

18) *A department that is well positioned politically is better able to influence its own course of action.* The politically positioned department has faculty placed in important senate and other campus committees, courses and programs tightly tied in with the course requirements of other major departments, donors, alumni, university board members, and political friends of the department, enrollment counts that are critical to the institutional health of the campus, and programs and faculty that are central

to the mission of the institution and/or that provide great positive visibility for the campus.

19) *The chair's personal political power is increased by his or her graceful, efficient productivity.* Chairs of departments that run smoothly and without much controversy are typically better received by administrators than are chairs of departments who produce boatloads of problems for higher-level administrators to deal with.

20) *Political power is increased by the perception of competence and excellence.* The chair can encourage this perception by being knowledgeable of the issues and competently resolving problems within the department.

21) *Political power is undermined by personal ambition.* Political power is increased by the perception that the individual's position is based upon the moral high ground and/or what is best for the overall institution as opposed to selfish parochial interests.

22) *Time changes every problem.* When first confronted with a problem, unless it is a critical matter of survival, take the time to study the issue. Over time, the cast of characters involved changes, the position held by constituents relevant to an issue also changes, and fiscal, political, and social factors vary from those that may have precipitated the problem. These changes may make resolution more possible. The savvy political leader constantly looks to align problems with new factors necessary for their resolution.

23) *Political position is often indicated by the information made available to whom and when individuals learn that information.* The earlier information is received, and the more direct the source, the greater one's potential political power, and the greater the likelihood that one will be able to influence a political agenda rather than be subject to or victim of someone else's decision.

24) *Don't play politics with people's lives.* Although the public nature of chairing necessitates that political ramifications be considered, remember that most decisions will affect the lives of your colleagues. Treat everyone on campus the same way that you would like to be treated.

25) *Never let them see you sweat.*

Questions to Consider

1) Analyze your department relative to the open systems perspective. What are the important constituent groups outside of the department's own faculty and staff? What does each group want from the department? What does each group have that the department could benefit from?

2) Choose the two most politically influential faculty members on your campus. Choose the two most politically influential central administrators on your campus. Choose the two most politically influential staff members on your campus. Why have your responded as you have?

3) What are the two or three most politically important documents that department chairs need to know on your campus? Explain your response.

4) Conduct an environmental scan of your department. What are two or three of the best opportunities available to the department? What are two or three of the biggest dangers facing the department? How much is your department responding to these opportunities and dangers?

5) Choose one important issue on your campus. Analyze the political blocks on the various sides of the issue. Who is in each political block?

6) Analyze your department's political position on campus. How well is it positioned relative to funding? Faculty positions? Information access? Decision-making influence?

BUDGET

Professor Maurice Penny has been a faculty member for 15 years and chair of the Department of Sociology for two years. In that time he has seen enrollments rise from 4,000 to 12,000 students. Recent years, how-ever, have seen reductions in the budget due to a state revenue decline. Dean Climber is in his first year, having been hired by Provost Dewey Moore, who is in his second year. The new dean has declared that all chairs will have to make a budget request for the following fiscal year. Funds will be allocated to departments based upon written documents and the formal presentation to the dean. Shifts between departments in funds and even vacant positions are possible. All chairs have been instructed to provide evidence of the efficiency of resource utilization as they lead to quality outcomes for students, the college, and the university. The dean has also stated that professional development is of the high-est priority in the future, and all chairs should endeavor to show how resources may be reallocated from other department uses to promote the growth of faculty scholarship, grants, and contract work. Chair Penny wonders how to approach the ominous fiscal year and his new dean.

Traditional academic culture values good work more highly than money. Yet we all know that good work requires funds invested in the faculty, staff, and students and their development, training, equipment, and supplies. It is the chair's responsibility to maximize the good that is done with the resources made available to the department. Enormous good can come from the application of large capital investments into productive facilities, but it can also come from the timely application of seed monies to fertilize the germination of faculty work during opportune periods of growth.

In a budget environment where there never seems to be enough of the pie to go around, it is the chair who is typically responsible for approving where the money will be spent in the department. Who will be paid to teach what classes? What equipment will be purchased? Who will receive professional development support at what level of funding? Chairs have increasingly been asked to assume duties of budget management. What should a chair know about the budget in order to be effective?

1) *Budgeting follows one of two models: decentralized—responsibility-based budgeting (also known as dollar-based budgeting)—or centralized—units receive the minimal funding necessary for operations and further allocations must be requested and approved by an external department authority.* Institutions vary widely as to customary budget practices. Chairs with little budget discretion are typically pass-through agents. These chairs don't decide where money is spent; instead they merely monitor money as it flows through their departments. In other instances, chairs exercise independence in their decisions as to how much and where department dollars are spent. They may be able to freely move money from one area (e.g., in personnel salaries) into another (e.g., professional development or to fund research needs). But this discretion typically requires that chairs be responsible for balancing the budget. Budgetary shortfalls in one year may lead to a department budget reduction the following year.

2) *Budgeting is a process of resource requests and allocation decisions that operates within a generally predictable timeframe.* Typically at the beginning of each academic year, department chairs learn of the allocation made available by the university (academic vice president and the vice president's budget officer and dean) for operation of the department. The decision as to how much money is available to departments results from a process that varies by institution. Some allocation decisions involve a great deal

of input, others ask for little department input. In some colleges and universities there are competitive allocation processes, in other schools a more formula driven process is the norm. In some schools upwards of 90% of the budget will go toward the salaries of tenured faculty, in other departments, there can be dramatic fluctuations in overall budget allocations dependent upon how much or little grant or other soft money is available.

3) *It is typically the chair's responsibility to oversee department expenditures.* The process of budget allocation varies with the normative practices and culture of the college and university. Some chairs will have almost all of their operations micromanaged by the dean or other administrative officer. Other chairs will have considerable freedom over how most of their department's money is spent.

4) *Budgeting can be viewed as a tremendously exciting opportunity, similar to investing for the future,* rather than a management chore equivalent to balancing the checkbook.

5) *Budgets have been described as an economic prediction, a political activity, an organizational plan, and a management control process.* Like any public document for complex organizations with multiple constituencies, the annual budget serves many functions. Most simply, it is an educated guess as to how much money the organization needs to function. But the budget is also a political tool in that it describes the organization's high and low priorities. It sends a message as to how much money will be spent on programs that will serve particular constituent groups. As an organizational plan, the budget shows year after year where the department is headed. As a management control process, the budget tells constituents both within and outside of the department what is expected of different parts of the department.

6) *Resource management is a fiduciary responsibility.* The chair serves as trustee over the resources of the department. Department resources in the way of facilities, equipment, and the like are entrusted to the chair to manage and oversee for the benefit of both current and future generations of students and faculty. The chair is responsible to serve as guardian over these resources.

7) *Good budgeting means many things.* It is important not to spend more than the department has been allocated. It is also at least equally important to spend all the money that the department has been allocated and to spend it where it will yield the greatest return to students and faculty. Department chairs need to know how much money they have and where that money is best spent. While it may be comforting to know that the department has not overspent, it is also important to know how much of the annual budget remains periodically throughout the fiscal year so that those funds can be spent as needed. It is important to avoid the "fire sale" mentality typical in bureaucracies on an annual budget system where there is a mad search for ways to spend the last dollars remaining before the fiscal year ends and central administration swallows up remaining balances. It is much better to know who needs money, when they need it, and which needs are prioritized highest.

8) *Break the budget down by categories* (and track funds each month of the fiscal year). This will help you understand your budget and how your department utilizes resources.

Expenditure Categories

- Personnel: Tenured, probationary, temporary full-time and part-time, teaching associates, graduate assistants, student workers, full-time and part-time staff

- Operating expenses: Phones, copying, paper, office supplies, etc.

- Professional development: Travel, honorarium, etc.

- Equipment: Maintenance, purchase, lease

Income Categories

- General fund: Money that comes from the general operating budget of the institution.

- External fund: Mostly money from external grants and contract work.

- Rollovers: Funds originally from a previous year's budget that are transferred into the next year's budget.

- Transfers: Money that comes from another unit on campus, or money transferred from one expense category (e.g., personnel dollars) to another category (e.g., professional development).

- Foundation accounts (including alumni accounts and endowment accounts): This is money that usually comes from another organization which, though allied with the university, is officially a separate business entity.

- Scholarship accounts: These are funds typically generated from fundraising and donations.

9) *Capital budgets earmarked for major construction and foundation or grant-generated soft money cannot usually be mixed with general operating money.* There are legal prohibitions against the co-mingling of money generated for a specific purpose such as construction of buildings or labs or for student scholarships. Such accounts are usually kept separately from general department operating accounts.

10) *Know the difference between budgets and end-of-year close-out reports.* A budget is a projection of how money will be spent. A year-end closeout report tells precisely how much and where money has been spent. Most departments spend money in predictable patterns; that is, X% on temporary faculty, Y% on copying, Z% on travel. The best predictor for how much money is needed next year is how much money has been spent the past year.

11) *To determine whether a particular allocation has been used most efficiently, triangulate the data to get multiple perspectives on how and why resources have been expended.* Ask the same budget question of a number of knowledgeable sources in the department, other departments, and other campuses.

12) *Department chairs are often expected to present budget requests for the next fiscal year.* Great care needs to be expended on this process. It is not merely the process of putting together a wish list. Budget requests are most powerful when they are reasonable and when they clearly demonstrate that efficient use of scarce resources will yield benefits to the department, college, and institution. Budget requests should follow through on per-

formance themes that consistently move the department's work year after year. For example, if a department's theme is service-learning, requesting additional funds to augment and build upon previously successful service-learning programs may be a very persuasive argument for additional funding.

13) *Budget persuasion is best achieved with hard evidence and thematic consistency among department, college, and university missions.* It is not enough just to say "we need this." It is important that chairs provide clear evidence that expenditures will lead to demonstrable results. The impact of this evidence is compounded when allocations lead to results consistent with the strategic mission of the college and university.

14) *In actual budget presentations, keep it simple.* Given the nature of bureaucracy, the further up the hierarchy a budget request travels, the less time decision-makers have to read long reports. Detailed evidence may be presented in summary form with appendices containing tables, graphs, and complicated data.

15) *The most important tool in the department chair's fiscal arsenal is credibility.* It is critical that the chair be believable. Credibility is just as important in the chair's relationship with the dean as it is in the chair's internal relations with faculty. Then, when chairs say that funds are necessary for program operation, the dean will know it is so.

16) *Careful budget management is facilitated by real-time, online reports.* Some units receive accounts of their expenditures and how much they have remaining in their annual appropriations in real time. Other departments will only receive budget information that is dated and that does not really reflect the state of the department's budget. Some chairs like to check department accounts daily, others like a hardcopy on their desks once a month.

17) *Monitor the rate of expenditures.* Expenditures typically fall in predictable patterns during the fiscal year. Follow each category of expenditure—personnel (full- and part-time), operating expenses such as copying and equipment maintenance, and professional development—as these budget categories are spent before classes begin, during the first few weeks of

class, at the term break, and during the beginning of the last academic term. To fully benefit from your resources, the chair needs to know how much there is left to spend.

18) *Calculate expenditures in a number of ways to determine how efficiently resources are used.* To understand how well your department is utilizing its resources, consider the following:

- Cost per FTES or section; while most cost is personnel, there may also be equipment and operating expenses

- Cost per major, or major FTES or section

- Cost per general education FTES or section

- Cost per elective FTES or section

- Cost per laboratory course FTES or section

- Cost of each of the above in each department program area

19) *Determine how success is defined in your department, and determine the best possible means of supporting those essential operations.* Is success defined as the lowest cost to the university per FTES? The largest number of majors? The highest pass rate on the national exam? The most grant money awarded? The most publications? Understand that this metric for success will vary between faculty, the dean, and other constituents.

20) *In a rational model, budget allocation decisions are based upon the criteria of academic quality, financial need, goal centrality, and relative cost.* Department chairs need to provide evidence of the high quality of their academic programs, how necessary finances are to the department's students and faculty, how much the department is central to the core mission of the institution, and how reasonable the department's costs are relative to other units and relative to the achievements of the department.

21) *Department allocation requests must take into consideration the college and institutional allocation perspective.* Many department chairs might like to argue that their unit is most important to the institution, but this is a parochial point of view that undermines the credibility of the chair. Other academic and nonacademic units of the institution will have legitimate budget needs. The chair should only make budget requests that are reasonable in light of the legitimate needs of others in the institution.

22) *Most faculty want more budget transparency.* The chair who lays out resource requests, allocations, and expenditures in a clear fashion will build support for the integrity of resource use in the department. Such important presentations encourage faculty to understand overall department operations so as to better equip the faculty for self-governance.

23) *Communication of the chair's expectations for department mission, goals, and outcomes will help faculty understand budget decisions.* If the chair bases allocation decisions on how well faculty production relates to the department's mission and goals, and if the faculty know what kind of measurable outcomes the chair sees as making progress toward the achievement of those goals and outcomes, then department members will better understand the allocation decisions the chair makes.

24) *Department-level resources may be centrally allocated or allocation may be decentralized to the program or faculty level.* Typically department chairs must sign off on expenditures. The actual decision of what to spend money on may be made by officers of the department or by chairs themselves. Chairs can appoint or hold elections in which program heads, associate chairs, and a budget committee of the faculty may be authorized to make or recommend budget decisions.

25) *Budget allocations are more likely to yield tangible results if coupled with action plans.* Action plans specify goals, the sequence of activities to be accomplished, the timeframe in which tasks will be accomplished, and who is responsible for accomplishments. Budget allocations made for programmatic improvement, faculty development, and curricular expansion may also need an action plan from the faculty who will receive the budget allocation. This action plan lets the chair know exactly how the expenditure will benefit the department, who will be responsible for the improvement, and when such improvements will take place.

26) *Budget decisions may be easy to make, but repercussions from these decisions may be difficult to weather.* Given a clear list of department goals, decisions about where to spend money may be easy to make. Faculty and staff who do not receive allocations, however, may make their displeasure known. It is important that the department understand the motivations behind budget decisions and that the budget process be transparent. While de-

partment members may disagree with the chair's judgment, there should be no question that decisions were made fairly and for well-intended reasons.

27) *Budgets are dynamic instruments in the sense that they are just a prediction of how money will be used.* For example, departments restricted by too many dollars in one account and too few dollars in another account may need to swap funds from one category with funds from another. It is important that departments maintain some historical perspective on how much money is typically spent in various budget categories. It is also wise to maintain a reserve to handle unforeseen department needs. Such reserves will allow the department to take advantage of unexpected opportunities as well.

28) *Get to know your budget officers.* Dependent upon the size of the institution, there are specified officers who draft budgets for decision-makers to consider. Who are those budget officers in the central administration? Is there a budget officer for your department assigned to your dean? What economic models do they use to do their planning and projections?

29) *What is your campus budget calendar?* When are allocations to academic affairs, specific colleges, and specific departments made? When are final spending reports due? For example, decisions about new faculty hires have to be made in time to factor them into spending allocation reports. Knowing when final accountings have to be made will also tell chairs something about when money that has not been used by other units may be available for some department need.

30) *Fundraising* has become a part of the chair's job description on some campuses. What should chairs consider relative to fundraising?

- *Why did Willie Sutton rob banks?* Since most colleges and universities have upwards of 90% of their department budgets in faculty salaries, chairs looking to capture funds for reallocation to other department needs may have to look at reducing personnel costs. Chairs able to convince their deans that all or a portion of the savings from reducing or combining sections, unpaid leaves, and full/partial retirements should go back to the department will have an enormous resource for professional development, student worker hires, equipment, seed money, and so on. To illustrate, by combining two sections of seven students into one section of fourteen, in a three-unit course, that might mean a reallocation of several thousand dollars to some other purpose.

- *Alumni calls.* Many departments are hiring their own students or even private call contacts to ring alumni and friends of the department to ask for donations. Often donations more than pay for the cost of making the calls, and even small donors tend to grow their contributions in the future.

- *Friend-making and fundraising.* Chairs need to know the difference between making money and making friends. Friend-making is just as important as making money since friends can provide political support and volunteer their time for department events. Ten hours volunteered to help a department can offset a $100–$200 fundraising expense. Friends can also say good things about the department. Donors tend to give to organizations known to be of high quality and that do good work.

- *Advisory boards.* A group of alumni and constituents serving on an advisory board can pay long-term dividends. Constituent feedback is important for accreditation. Advisory boards are also the foundation of fundraising campaigns by providing labor, contacts, and advice.

- *Grants.* Residual money that comes to departments from success in competitive and sole-source grants often goes to discretionary accounts of inestimable value to chairs. Dependent upon the grant, residuals can amount to and exceed 50% of the total grant. With this money graduate students can be hired, functions can be catered, and faculty can even make extra salary.

- *Contracts.* Contracts for services can purchase faculty time on an annual or longer-term basis. They can provide training opportunities for students and connect junior faculty to important constituents. Contracts also do good work for important groups that the institution should serve.

- *Faculty teaching in other departments.* One way to enhance the budget is to allow other campus departments to buy some teaching time from your faculty. So long as your own department is able to fulfill its curricular obligations, faculty teaching in other departments can free up otherwise allocated personnel dollars.

- *Development infrastructure as a pre-condition.* Fundraising does not typically happen unless there is an established infrastructure of development personnel who can handle donor research, the logistics of grant proposals, the necessary notices and thank-you correspondence, the accounting of scholarship, endowments, or other contributions, and help faculty who secure grants or contracts.

- *Contact lists.* Who is allowed to call whom? Chairs who have hot leads on possible donors need to coordinate with their own development office. The last thing a friend of the institution and possible donor needs are multiple calls from different people on the same campus, all asking for money for different purposes. Successful fundraising requires knowledge of who is most likely to be successful when they ask.

- *Money follows a purpose.* Chairs are as generous as the next person. Are you willing to give money when you don't have confidence that it will be used well? Whether it is grants, contracts, endowments, scholarships, or other money the department wants, it is always the case that donors want to know that the money will be used well. That usually means the department needs to have a track record of having the personnel, programs, and policies in place that will efficiently translate a donation into something positive for the students, faculty, or society.

- *Fundraisers tend to be most effective when they passionately believe in the organization they are trying to raise resources to support.* Do the unit's fundraisers know the organization's story? Its history, purpose, and the mission that makes it unique? Do they convey this institutional story passionately enough to make contributing to that organization attractive to potential donors?

QUESTIONS TO CONSIDER

1) On a scale from 1 to 5 (1 = little incentive; 5 = great deal of incentive), how much incentive do you feel the department chairs on your campus have to save money? Explain your response. How could department chairs on your campus be given greater incentive to most efficiently utilize resources?

2) If a department on your campus has a faculty member completely buy out his or her time with grant money, where does that faculty member's salary go for that budget year?

3) If a department on your campus saves salary dollars by combining sections of the same course, does that department get to reallocate the dollars that have been saved? Can the chair reallocate that money for professional development?

4) How much of the department budget do you believe chairs should be responsible for? Explain your response.

5) Choose a department on your campus to analyze. How centralized/decentralized is its budget and allocation process?

6) Identify two or three departments on your campus that produce a large number of enrollments at low cost. Now identify two or three departments on your campus that produce a small number of enrollments at high cost. Why is there such a difference in cost per enrollment? Is the difference justifiable?

7) What percentage of your department's budget is spent in each of the following categories of expenditures: personnel (tenure track, nontenure track full- and part-time, student workers), operating expenses (phones, copying, supplies), professional development, equipment purchase and maintenance, other?

8) If you as a chair were authorized by your dean to reallocate any salary savings made available as a result of an unexpected, unpaid leave, what percentage of the $60,000 would you allocate to professional development? Support of teaching and learning? Other support? Why?

8

DEPARTMENT MEETINGS

Professor Jake Speare has been recently elected chair of the Department of Theatre with lukewarm faculty support. He is about to face his first department meeting of the year. It is also the first formal faculty gathering since the last department meeting one year ago. Frankly, meetings were avoided because they seemed to stir up too many problems, and emotional outbursts derailed discussion. When issues came to a vote, the lack of consensus made action difficult. One problem was that the faculty didn't feel they understood issues well enough to make informed choices. Too much time was spent on administrivia, and faculty complained that they couldn't attend because of classes and other professional commitments. Then there is Professor Wrench, who makes it a point to comment on every subject and who is very fond of making motions. Every one of his positions is opposed by a group of faculty led by Professor Stuch. Their tangling consumes so much time that little is accomplished.

How should a new chair deal with department meetings? In this age of electronic communications, are they even necessary? If they are important, what is the best way for chairs to approach these gatherings of the faculty?

For most academic units, the department meeting is the only regularly scheduled opportunity for the faculty (and in some cases, for the staff) to personally interact as a body. Meeting times and dates are preestablished at the beginning of each academic term or held on rotating days to include as many faculty as possible by accommodating as many schedules as possible. Faculty may view meetings as critical pieces of a schedule for action, or they may avoid them because of the conflicts that can engulf fractious parties cloistered together in the same room.

In most departments, it is the chair who calls for a meeting of the department and who sets the agenda. This is a considerable source of influence that should not be underestimated. It is typically the chair who introduces and moderates discussion and who commands the floor, recognizes speakers, and enables actions to be taken as a result of department deliberations. While email has added to department communications, electronic means cannot completely replace personal interaction. Face-to-face meetings remain necessary for emotional support and a sense of group support. Chairs must understand, however, that before the department meeting is held, it is important to consider the setting, the agenda, the nature of the business to be conducted, and the probable reactions of those in the meeting. Given a moderate-size faculty, an hour department meeting costs thousands of dollars of professional time. The chair must recognize just how important this time is to the faculty in the room, and to the institution, and to make the best use of the department meeting.

1) *The chair's performance in department meetings provides an opportunity to convey a public face that reflects the values and abilities of the chair.* Is the chair fair, respectful, knowledgeable, reasonable, capable, and a good representative of the department? Given the small number of times that professionals typically spend with all of their colleagues, the department meeting is the most critical social engagement for the department chair. How he or she frames questions objectively and insightfully, recognizes speakers without political or personal bias, and summarizes discussion so as to engender the next best step for the department speaks volumes for the chair's character and competency. Department chairs who allow themselves to be dragged into the mud of personal recriminations are less effective leaders than chairs who empathize with those making a comment but who are able to stay above the fray.

2) *The chair establishes the agenda for department meetings.* Most department policy manuals specify that it is the chair who leads meetings. The usefulness or uselessness of a meeting is largely dependent upon the efficiency with which the chair plans and runs the meeting. Are only issues important to most of the faculty on the agenda, or should items of less significance be handled in committees and reported as information items? Does the chair recognize what is of interest to most faculty and what requires full discussion before the legitimacy of some action on behalf of the department is accepted?

3) *The chair's position as moderator of discussion is critical to department relations and to forward a department agenda.* Chairs must be knowledgeable on the issues, unbiased, good listeners, capable summarizers of discussion, and turn department approval into action. Good moderators know when discussion is necessary and also when it is just continuing to beat a dead horse.

4) *Chairs are responsible for providing the background information and laying out viable options for the faculty to consider before deciding upon a course of action.* Because the department chair has access to personnel files, privileged data sources, and the offices of the dean and other central administrators and their staff, chairs are best equipped to research some issue of importance to the department. It is essential that the faculty be given the information they need to consider before engaging in data-driven discussion. For example, prior to consideration of how to absorb a budget reduction, faculty need a clear presentation on the department's fiscal condition, models for budget reduction, and ramifications of each model if adopted. Does the chair present background information and options for department actions in an unbiased fashion? Is the chair knowledgeable on the issue? Does the chair have the confidence of those with information important to the department, so he or she can gather the information most necessary for the department to know?

5) *In a 10-FTEF department, a one-hour meeting costs roughly $1,000–$2,000 in personnel costs.* What does this mean in concrete terms?

- Use every precious minute as efficiently as possible.

- Overhead and PowerPoint presentations need to be clear and work the first time.

- All faculty should receive an electronic agenda before the meeting and a hardcopy at the meeting.

- As much as possible, housekeeping and administrivia need to be taken care of at some time other than the department meeting.

6) *Regularity of meetings varies by department.* Some departments meet only when there is business to conduct. Others meet every other week. Still others meet once a month. It is critical that all relevant constituencies be able to attend department meetings. If meetings to talk about tenure and promotion criteria are only held early in the morning when senior faculty are available, this scheduling may exclude the junior faculty who teach during the earlier hours of the day and who have significant interests in this topic.

7) *Pay attention to meeting ambience.* Human communication is primarily nonverbal. The type of language employed, even seating arrangements, can speak volumes. Is the department meeting to be formal or informal? Business efficient or warm and friendly? Will refreshments be provided or maybe faculty will take turns bringing goodies? On some occasions maybe a meeting will even be catered! Coffee, juice, and muffins are very much appreciated during early morning meetings. This tells the faculty that they are valued.

8) *Meeting minutes are the official record of department actions and agreements.* Minutes need to be taken by an unbiased party, sent to the department for review, approved as officially accepted at the following meeting, and then recorded as a department archive. While some minutes may look like narratives of who said what, at a minimum, minutes are a history of department actions. In future years when disagreements may call for research into the intent of a department vote, the minutes will be consulted.

9) *Do department committees regularly report their action and discussion items, or are paper or electronic minutes distributed to the faculty?* Faculty committees work on behalf of the faculty. Except in the case of confidential

personnel committee work, all faculty have a right to know what their committees are doing. In the name of transparency of operations, it is typically the best policy to routinely send out meeting agendas and minutes. Another reason to send out email accounts of committee actions is because faculty time is so expensive. It is always best to reduce the amount of time spent reporting during department meetings by sending out information via email. Discussion of significant committee actions may also be in the best interests of the department. If the chair feels that discussion and consideration of committee actions is important, then it is appropriate to invest department meeting time to do so.

10) *Reserve some time for public kudos and recognition of faculty and staff achievements.* All departments are human organizations. Recognition of significant publications, grants, teaching awards, and the like presents models for emulation by all members of the department. We all need a pat on the back now and then.

11) *Become familiar with* Robert's Rules of Order. Academic departments are always changing, and while change is welcomed by some, it will inevitably be resisted by others. Discourse requires rules for engagement; therefore, it is imperative that the chair be familiar with *Robert's Rules of Order* (Robert, Evans, Honemann, & Balch, 2000) due to the widespread legitimacy of its application in academic organizations. Some departments elect a parliamentarian and some do not. It is important for the chair who moderates discussion to know the rules of order—who speaks when and on which subjects? What is a point of clarification? What is a point of order? How does a motion come to a vote? When is it proper to begin a speakers list? When should the chair excuse himself or herself from the role of moderator and appoint a temporary moderator?

12) *Be willing to employ a speakers list, especially while discussing contentious issues.* A list of who has raised their hands to speak ensures civil engagement, maintains order, and permits all of those with something to say an opportunity to take the floor from those who are perhaps louder, more vocal, and insistent. Use of a speakers list helps keep discussions on track and minimize emotional outbursts that can derail a meeting.

13) *For issues that can benefit from further study and deliberation, consider employing study groups* or assign research to standing or ad hoc committees to pick up where discussions end. It is important that chairs recognize when discussion is becoming circular and unproductive or when discussion of one topic threatens to monopolize the time allocated for other department meeting items. At such a time it may be useful to table discussion, elect, appoint, or call for volunteers to serve on a group to research and discuss the contentious issue, and then report back to the chair and faculty. The charge and the schedule can be provided to the newly formed committee during the department meeting or in later discussion with the chair. Also be sure to appoint someone to convene the first meeting of the group.

14) *It is critical that committees represent department constituencies well enough that the committee has credibility.* All department meeting activities need to take place in a transparent fashion so as to minimize perceptions of unfair process. The process through which department committees are nominated and elected is critical to department health. If elections take place during department meetings, all constituents need to know when the election will take place and the means used to nominate and elect committee members. Discontent is guaranteed by committees that are loaded with too many advocates of one position.

15) *Employ techniques to further progress on contentious issues.* Invite faculty input via department listserv, or invite written comments that will be used to revise documents for further department consideration.

16) *Employ action plans to move along important department decisions.* The department meeting that leads to a motion carried but does not lead to action is like a promise broken. It is up to the chair to enable action on the will of the department by helping the department develop a concrete plan of action, with measurable indicators of progress to be achieved within a specified timeframe by specified representatives of the department. Talk needs to be translated into action.

17) *When the chair clearly has a position on some issue, it is appropriate to temporarily appoint someone else to lead discussion.* The perception of the chair as objective is perhaps the most critical requirement for the job. The chair

who can see both sides of an issue, who can summarize opposing points of view, and who does not take sides can be an effective broker in the department. If the chair has a point of view on some issue in the department, it may be best for the chair to temporarily hand over the responsibility of running the meeting to the associate chair or some other senior member of the department. Doing so allows the chair to express his or her point of view while remaining objective and evenhanded on all other issues.

18) *Faculty expected to contribute a briefing or report at department meetings need to be advised beforehand so that they will be prepared in advance.* It is important that a culture of excellence be created in the department. This is especially true during public displays and presentation of faculty work. Chairs will often want heads of committees to report. They may want a faculty members to highlight their work or for a staff member to present findings from institutional research conducted on behalf of the department. In every case involving public presentation, it is wise to make sure that the speaker clearly knows what the chair wants presented and how long the presentation should take. If overheads or PowerPoint presentations are to be used, the chair may even request to review the materials to ensure that they will be effectively presented. Contributors should also know when they will be asked to speak, whether they will be asked to field questions, and the context of the item they will address relative to the positions of those in the meeting.

QUESTIONS TO CONSIDER

1) Choose two or three administrators with different leadership styles who have chaired meetings that you have attended. Describe the differences in the styles that they displayed during meetings.

2) What *Robert's Rules of Order* are most important for chairs to be familiar with?

3) For the next meeting you attend, calculate how much it is costing in the way of personnel salaries.

4) List the department business that can be best taken care of via email.

5) List the department business that needs to be taken care of in person.

Time Management

Professor I. M. Runnin is the new chair of the Department of Organic Engineering. Having been on the job for three months already, he still doesn't feel as if he has his feet on the ground (although he is careful who he will admit this to). The previous two chairs of the department were basically place holders who were in the chair's position as acting for just one year stints. While Chair Runnin wants to do his best to serve his colleagues, he wonders how other chairs are able to get their reports in on time, how they have the time to attend to the dean's emails, take care of faculty and student problems, do the planning, scheduling, and reviews, serve on committees, and represent the department. He doesn't know where his time goes, but he doesn't have enough of it. Whenever he gets caught up, some new problem gets in the way. His own teaching is suffering. Forget about his scholarship. There doesn't seem to be an end in sight to this whirlwind.

Perhaps the biggest difference between being a faculty member and a department chair is how time is spent. For many department chairs, their schedules are in charge of them. So much of the chair's time is spent on the bureaucratic grind (preparation for and response to requests for information and reports) and the household routine (scheduling, recruiting, managing the budget and staff, and working on student needs and complaints) that little time is left for leadership, research, or life outside of work (Chu & Veregge, 2002).

For a newly minted department chair formerly accustomed to the splendid isolation of the lab or office, the scarcity of time truly makes it more precious. What should be considered as chairs try to successfully manage their work time?

1) *Perspective first: Chairing is a public role versus faculty work that is largely private.* Although it is natural to reminisce about the good old days when time moved more slowly, it is important for chairs to recognize that theirs is a new role that they have elected to accept.

2) *Perspective second: The chair's day is less predictable than the faculty day.* Crises happen at the least opportune moments.

3) *It takes time for new chairs to get their feet on the ground.* The chair position brings unfamiliarity, which means chairs need time to learn, time to try, and time to adjust.

4) *Prioritize.* Because chairs are at the neck of the bureaucratic hourglass, they receive from above and below their middle-management level more reports, requests, and demands that they can deal with each day. Chairs have to prioritize that which is most important and attend to those items first. Experienced administrators perform schedule triage; they scan the day's demands, determine what must be dealt with immediately for fear of death or incarceration, what needs to be dealt with but can wait, and that which really isn't worth much time. A good source of information for what can wait and what can't are experienced chairs on campus who are recognized as masters of the craft.

5) *Get an associate chair.* In departments of ten or more FTEF, it may be useful to appoint or elect an associate chair. The associate chair serves many functions, including drafting documents, chairing selected committees, attending some meetings on behalf of the chair, and administrative data collection. Appointment of an associate chair also provides a spot for up-and-coming leadership of the department to learn the craft of chairing. If the position is rotated periodically, it also gives more faculty the opportunity to know what it's like to spend so much time doing so much for others.

6) *Delegate report drafting/writing* to senior faculty, emeritus faculty, executive council members, or the associate chair to first draft and then modify reports based on your directions. While chairing is a service position, it is not a slave position. All departments have to write self-study or accreditation reports. Why not delegate the job of drafting these time-consuming documents to an experienced hand? This faculty member may be compensated by some small stipend, consulting fee, or assigned time. However, remember to work closely with the report drafter to minimize the chances that the report will yield unexpected surprises.

7) *Delegate the drafting of course schedules* to an associate chair or program head. Anyone who has done course scheduling knows that it can consume all available time. To best schedule, room capacities and facilities need to be checked. Is there enough student demand to warrant a bigger room? If so, can the request be made early enough to reserve an adequate space with the proper facilities? Is a time change warranted? After checking with students as to when a course needs to be rescheduled, is the faculty member available to teach at that new hour? How do proposed schedule changes in your department work with feeder courses from other departments? Is there conflict or can a new time be worked out that is agreeable to everyone? Do any of the faculty have research time buy-outs or leaves that will necessitate schedule juggling? Have all the faculty been queried about schedule changes they would like to make? Whoever is in charge of drafting the schedule needs to meet with the faculty to discuss potential changes and relate the discussions to the chair, who typically signs off on the schedule before it is forwarded to central administration or the dean.

8) *Appoint advisors from faculty and advanced students.* Almost all advising takes the form of a question-and-answer session and is rather routine. Some chairs have student advising in their roster of duties. Most advising questions can be answered by bright students and experienced faculty. Then only the most pressing problems can be forwarded to the chair.

9) *Allow staff to help you lead by requesting specific information at regular, predictable times* so that you have the information you need to get ahead of problems rather than engage in fire drills following unanticipated situ-

ations. You know that the budget is going to be an issue. Having a weekly budget printout delivered every Monday morning is one way to make sure you stay abreast of the problem. Experienced staff are able to process much more information than ever before. Chairs who can construct important questions to be researched by their staff will be more successful than chairs who just see the same old problems and the same old answers (or lack of answers).

10) *Archived documents provide a ready guide for the production of new documents.* Don't waste time trying to reinvent the wheel. In almost every case, for every report that needs to be written, there are previously prepared reports to serve as reference. For an accreditation report, for example, there are not only reports previously prepared by the chair's own department, but there are reports available from other departments, and even from other colleges and universities. A good source of information will be administrators who oversee these reports for your institution. Ask them what departments, colleges, and universities have prepared excellent reports that can be modeled.

11) *Before the beginning of each academic year, develop a list of what reports are due when.* Knowing when reports are due allows chairs to plan and budget their own time and the time of their staff and faculty. Chairs can task staff and others to whom they can delegate responsibility to collect and analyze data, and draft reports/documents in advance of those deadlines.

12) *Maintain your own calendar.* Some chairs schedule their Microsoft Outlook calendars exclusively. Others like their administrative assistant to maintain their calendars. Whatever you choose, it is OK to reserve blocks of time for your own use.

13) *It's OK to turn off the phone and computer monitor for periods of time.*

14) *Not every demand on your time needs to be immediately addressed.* Part of the craft of leadership is knowing when a problem is important enough, clearly defined enough, and there is enough information to form an acceptable resolution. Resolving a problem in the short term sometimes just creates bigger problems in the long term. Jumping to every loud noise is too tiring for the long run.

15) *Protect the faculty's time as zealously as you guard your own.* The faculty's time is just as important as the chair's time. If you have an appointment with the faculty, be on time. If you're running unexpectedly late, give the faculty the option of rescheduling, rather than expect them to wait for a meeting for an unknown amount of time.

16) *No matter how rushed you feel inside, you don't have to show it outside.* Whoever you have decided to spend time with deserves all of your attention and focus. Make sure they know that from how you behave with them. Don't be looking over their shoulders for the next meeting.

QUESTIONS TO CONSIDER

1) What reports do chairs regularly need to prepare on your campus? When do they need to be prepared and when are they due?

2) What reports should be drafted for the chair by someone else? What reports need to be the chair's work in their entirety?

3) What information do chairs need to have regularly prepared by staff for their review? How often do chairs need to see each piece of information?

10

PERSONNEL EVALUATION AND PERFORMANCE COUNSELING

Professor Fair is in her first year as chair of the Department of Measurement and Statistics, and she is about to write her first personnel evaluation. The department has been undergoing a dramatic revitalization, with many faculty retirements and replacements with high-quality Ph.D.s. Although she has been a personal friend of Professor Shirley Lamb, Chair Fair still feels capable of doing a quality evaluation report. She knows that Professor Lamb has been having personal problems that have prevented her from realizing the enormous potential she demonstrated upon hire. Chair Fair wonders how much to make of the personal issues and how much to evaluate the performance or lack of performance of the faculty member undergoing evaluation. After looking at Professor Lamb's personnel file, it appears that previous evaluations have been very kind in the sense that they rationalized the lack of achievement in teaching and scholarship by saying that personal issues would end and the evaluations of performance would inevitably improve. The dean's reviews, on the other hand, have consistently called for more professional achievement in teaching and scholarship. Chair Fair's report is due in two weeks and will have a great impact on tenure and promotion decisions.

Most department chairs have served on committees evaluating their colleagues for retention, tenure, and promotion. As department chair, however, evaluations typically bear a different weight. On some campuses, chairs write their own reports separate from the department committee's report. The chair's evaluation can determine whether colleagues retain their jobs, get raises, or are released. Unlike the central administrator, the chair sees most of the department faculty every day. And someday soon, the chair will become faculty once more and reside down the hall from a colleague on whom the chair has passed judgment.

As difficult as evaluation of one's colleagues may be, it is, nevertheless, a requirement of professionalism. It is easy to rationalize and say "I'm not an administrator, and I'm not paid to judge my peers." In reality, a justification like this only passes the buck. Responsibility is passed onto central administrators without the benefit of an important review from the faculty side of the house. The department chair sits in the transitional position between faculty and administration. Chairs are uniquely qualified to evaluate faculty since they are so much more familiar with the faculty, their work, their relationships with colleagues, and everyday interactions with students and staff. Like medical doctors and lawyers, the faculty are professionals who have been given the responsibility of knowing enough so that only they may judge their peers. That moral responsibility, plus the fiduciary responsibility and knowledge that a tenure decision is a multimillion dollar commitment, argues strongly for the importance of the department chair's evaluations of faculty and staff.

1) *On some campuses it is retention, tenure, and promotion policy that faculty will have the burden of proof on them.* On some Research I campuses, faculty may have to demonstrate that they are one of the world's experts on some area of study. On other campuses, good teaching may be sufficient for tenure and promotion. Whatever the required level of proof for tenure and promotion, it is clearly in the best interests of all concerned that faculty and staff be kept up to date as to where the chair sees their performance relative to expected standards of achievement in the department.

2) *Performance counseling should accompany personnel evaluation.* It is the responsibility of the personnel committee and the chair to provide faculty and staff under review with updates several times each year on their performance. In this way faculty and staff are advised as to how they can perform better relative to department standards. A dialogue ensues rather than a concluding report that terminates discussion at that level. Performance counseling aligns better with a philosophy that sees all members of the department as peers, each assisting the other to do their best job. See Higgerson (1996) for more information on performance counseling.

3) *Remember that a personnel evaluation is a legal document.* Anything that is written in the report may become public. Chairs are strongly encouraged to fully understand the policies that govern personnel evaluations and the interpretation of key terms such as *excellent, good,* and *adequate* as they apply to teaching and scholarship.

4) *The results of personnel evaluations should not be a surprise.* This is especially important relative to evaluation for tenure and promotion. Annual reviews should develop a case, consistently presented over the years, for the approval or denial of tenure or promotion.

5) *Make performance counseling a year-round (not just yearly) activity.* Helping colleagues improve their performance is a group objective. Assessments and concrete suggestions can contribute to a culture of improvement in the entire academic unit.

6) *Make job performance expectations clear.* It is critical that expectations for performance are clear so that there are no questions about what is expected. Concrete is much better than abstract. Specific must take the place of general expectations. If two publications are expected per year, in what journals? Do they need to be in print by review time or just accepted? How will anyone know what good teaching is compared to great teaching?

7) *Link evaluative comments to specific examples.* To further clarify observations and suggestions for the improvement of performance, punctuate counseling with specific behavioral illustrations. If a faculty member is told to improve teaching performance, what illustration can make this

clearer? If a staff member is told to improve service to students, what does this mean?

8) *Performance goals are annual milestones* to be reached by faculty and staff undergoing performance counseling. Make performance goals specific and manageable so that all parties know where the reviewee stands at any point in time.

9) *Establish a timeframe for achieving goals.* Goals for scholarship, teaching, and service should be linked to specific calendar periods. This will help reviewees better plan their work, and the department can better plan for its utilization of resources.

10) *Expectations for performance need to be linked to the resources required to get the job done.* Reviewees and department leadership need to discuss and agree on these mutual expectations immediately upon hire, followed by periodic reviews and adjustments of mutual expectations.

11) *Personnel evaluations should be written with third-person clarity and avoid disciplinary jargon.* Remember that any written performance counseling documents may be referred to for years to come. They may also be reviewed by those unfamiliar with a specific discipline's jargon. Always err on the side of too much detail as opposed to too little.

12) *Focus evaluative comments on the person's performance, not personality.* Performance counseling focuses on observable behaviors. Comments about character are inappropriate in the process of performance reviews unless they directly impact the productivity of faculty scholarship, teaching, or service.

13) *Make model documents and personnel files available.* Help the faculty prepare the best file possible in support of retention, tenure, and promotion by providing models that they can emulate. Ask faculty who have developed their own excellent personnel files to make them available for inspection by other faculty about to be reviewed. Have a group or individual discussion with faculty so they know what the chair expects to go into a good personnel file.

14) *Remember that you have a responsibility to listen.* Evaluations can be a source of anxiety for anyone undergoing review. It is the chair's respon-

sibility to listen to the reviewee even if what he or she has to say may be unpleasant. No one should tolerate abuse, but faculty and staff need to know that what they respectfully say matters enough that the chair will listen.

Questions to Consider

1) How should department personnel committees and chairs operate to minimize the possibilities of unpredictable evaluation outcomes? Explain your response.

2) How much consensus exists in your department relative to what it takes to be tenured and/or promoted? Explain your response.

3) On your campus, how much difference in performance is expected between assistant professors and full professors?

4) Are the professional development needs of full professors treated the same way as are the needs of assistant professors? Why or why not?

11

CHALLENGING PERSONNEL

Dr. Kush is a professor in the Department of English. Her genteel and refined manner, along with her excellent rapport with students and faculty, made her a real asset to the department. In recent years, however, Dr. Kush has been frequently and unexplainably absent from class. She has not attended social functions or department meetings. Students have complained that she does not hold her posted office hours or respond to their calls or emails, but she has a strong emotional support group within the department who cover for her when she is late or absent from class. Dr. Kind is chair of English and she cares deeply about the welfare of her colleagues, but she also knows that Dr. Kush's students have not been well served by her absences and lack of engagement.

Professor Lyon is difficult to be around. For as long as anyone can recall, he has been negative, sarcastic, and self-serving. He appears to derive pleasure from making other people's lives difficult. He spreads baseless rumors in the halls, hogs the floor in department meetings with his rants, clogs up progress in committees, and gives the entire department a detrimental image on campus with his public misbehavior. For some reason, though, he has his supporters on campus who believe his stories. Previous chairs have tried to rein him in and talk reason, but Professor Lyon has

threatened to grieve and sue whoever "deprives him of his rights." Newly
elected to the position of chair is Professor Lamb, who must determine
how she should deal with Professor Lyon.

Faculty and staff scenarios such as these are not uncommon. Challenging
faculty can be difficult because they are not involved enough, or because they
are too involved in affairs that are not their concern. For every Lyon, there
is a newly elected Lamb. How can department leaders approach personnel
problems such as this? First, it is important to understand that difficult personnel come in many different stripes. Some are problematic because they to-
tally withdraw from all department life; for that matter, they may even barely
come to work. There may be substance abuse issues and matters of personal
health and safety. On the other end of the spectrum are those faculty and
staff who are omnipresent in everyone's lives whether they should be involved
or not. They do not recognize boundaries of propriety, good form, and may
even step over the line into unethical or immoral behavior. A particularly
troublesome variant of this problematic faculty and staff person is the bully.
A bully is someone who employs power as well as coercion to get his or her
own way to the detriment of others.

In all of these cases, it is the chair who is first responsible for seeing to
it that the department and its work do not suffer. The chair has a fiduciary
responsibility that the faculty and staff do their jobs on behalf of the students
and the institution. Furthermore, chairs are the frontline officers charged
with protecting the rights of those in the department and seeing to it that
unethical and immoral behavior does not occur on their watch. When faced
with difficult faculty and/or staff, what should a chair consider?

1) *A problem to whom?* Personnel who are labeled difficult may not be problematic for everyone. For whom is that faculty or staff member difficult?
   Why does that person have such difficulty with that faculty or staff member? Chairs need to try to understand the personnel situation as best they
   can before deciding on a course of action (or inaction).

2) *Everyone has rights.* Even faculty, staff, and students who make life difficult for everyone have their legal rights. There are rights to due process,
   First Amendment rights, rights specified by the American Association

of University Professors, and basic human rights such as respect. It is the chair's responsibility to protect the rights of challenging personnel as much as anyone else in the department.

3) *Consult human resources.* They are the pros on your campus who have the experience and clout to help you out. They have been through this kind of thing before. Never act alone.

4) *Make sure your dean knows what is going on.* Always include the dean in the loop. This is especially crucial when there are problems that may find their way to the dean or beyond the dean to the offices of central administration. A dean who is surprised by something he or she should have been advised about is an unhappy dean.

5) *Have individual discussions with challenging personnel to get their point of view.* No matter how difficult it may be, chairs need to arrange personal individual discussions with the problematic faculty or staff member and those negatively affected by that person. Everyone has their own human story, and in this postmodern world we have multiple realities. For each individual, that reality is real enough for them to act. Spend the hours necessary to try to understand. If the chair is able to get to the bottom of things, fine. If the chair is unable to get to the bottom of things, he or she has at least shown a willingness to listen to each person's human story. The chair's validation of the legitimacy of individual perceptions will be useful in itself.

6) *Build a case.* For good reason, personnel actions take a substantial amount of evidence showing patterns of behavior consistent over time. It takes a great deal of effort over an extended period of time to build a case for personnel action. Evidence of behaviors in violation of established policy works best when it is substantiated evidence. When multiple eyes have witnessed inappropriate actions on the part of a problem faculty or staff member, then it is more likely that that evidence will bolster a case for personnel action.

7) *Taking notes.* What is your campus human resources policy on taking personal notes of meetings? Evidence of who said what to whom and when may be important in a personnel case. But remember that notes may be

subpoenaed. Is it best to keep a brief journal to help you recall the details of what happened, or should you keep a detailed diary?

8) *Bullies.* Recent research about bullies on playgrounds is relevant to the faculty or staff member who bullies others in the academic department. Especially for the civilized person who was taught to treat others as they would like to be treated, those who use their power to coerce others present an unfamiliar problem that is especially difficult to deal with. Bullies who are confronted early about their inappropriate behaviors stand the best chance of ceasing or altering their behaviors. To continue to allow bullies to take advantage of others just encourages bad behavior.

9) *How can the department help?* Faculty and staff who are especially problematic may be calling for help. Their intrusions into the private lives of others, and the salience that they demand, may be a very unfortunate call for attention.

10) *Professional help.* Most department chairs are not professional counselors, social workers, or therapists. Chairs need to know when professional help is called for and who to ask for confidential assistance.

11) *Enhance their self-image and self-esteem.* If the root of the problems exhibited by challenging faculty or staff has to do with that person's own self-image, what can the chair do to enhance that person's self-esteem? Are there assignments appropriate for that person to undertake that can be completed well enough for that person to receive praise?

12) *Find how they can contribute.* Everyone has their own talents. How can the talents of faculty or staff who have presented problems for the department be utilized to benefit the unit? Look at the department strategic plan. Develop a range of projects that the challenging faculty or staff member can undertake to contribute to the department.

13) *Build support groups.* Support groups of faculty or staff may be found within the department, on campus, or in the community. Are there friends or colleagues who can provide emotional or technical support and who are respected by the faculty or staff member having problems?

14) *Bolster your defenses.* If you decide that your department has a problem that requires action, prepare to be attacked. The most important support will come from the chair's colleagues in the department, the dean, and central administrators. If a bully is going over your head by pleading his or her case to an administrator, make sure that administrators know who they are dealing with and what the issues are.

15) *Expect the unexpected.* Problem personnel are especially difficult because they are so good at it. They are much better at causing problems than chairs usually are. Chances are the chair was elected to that position because he or she didn't create problems. Chairs need to learn to think like the problematic personnel. Doing so will help the chair anticipate the next problem the person may cause and develop a contingency plan to deal with it.

16) *Get the evidence.* Talk to colleagues and friends to find out what is going on in the life of the faculty or staff member who is having serious problems. Get to the roots of the issues causing personnel to exhibit problematic behavior. Triangulate by asking multiple sources for their view of the problem. But don't just settle for hearsay. You may have to look into the medical, legal, and/or ethical issues associated with some condition to determine the best course for you as department chair. Faculty and staff who have problems in their professional and/or personal lives can only get help if someone cares enough to do the homework necessary to understand. At the same time, however, faculty and staff in your department are entitled to privacy. But when their personal issues negatively impact the work of the department, then those otherwise personal issues may become relevant to the work of the chair.

17) *Is drug or alcohol abuse involved?* Even professionals can suffer from substance abuse. Faculty or staff may miss classes, not show up for appointments, ride an emotional rollercoaster, and exhibit erratic behavior. These are all symptoms of substance abuse. Chairs will need professional help coping with these issues. Remember, too, that friends of substance abusers usually do not want to turn on the person having problems. Friends of substance abusers see themselves as supporting the faculty or staff member who is addicted to drugs or alcohol. These "friends" actually encour-

age the abuse by covering or rationalizing for their colleague and friend. It will take some doing on the part of a chair to get the assistance of these people to help the abuser to face his or her drug or alcohol dependency.

18) *Legal considerations.* Faculty or staff who are difficult to be around is one thing. There is no law against being gruff or unfriendly. But behavior that is dangerous or abusive of students or colleagues cannot be tolerated. Immediate action needs to be taken to remedy a situation caused by problematic faculty or staff if the rights of others are trampled upon or if there is an unsafe condition that needs to be corrected. Is the professor able to supervise the chemistry lab? Can he or she keep a watchful eye out for the lab's inherent dangers?

   While attempting to deal with problematic faculty or staff, make sure that their rights are also respected. *Due process* is a legal term with campus-specific definitions usually found in faculty bylaws or in human resources policy documents.

19) *To respond or not to respond?* Difficult people sometimes try to evoke a response with some provocation. It's a power play of sorts to see if they can get you to leap if they tell you to jump. It's also a way for them to throw you off your game so that they can feel a sense of control by manipulating you. Calm in the face of provocation is usually the best approach. It shows that you are in charge of your life and your environment. For their own benefit, this may be what the difficult faculty member needs to see.

20) *When something must be done in the face of recurring problems, always try counseling* before negative disciplinary actions that will be recorded in the faculty or staff member's confidential personnel file.

21) *Employ a range of possible tactical responses.* When faced with challenging personnel who do not respond to counseling, reason, or patience, there are a number of alternative actions.

   • *Wait them out.* Usually the first tactic a chair should employ is to see if time will take care of problematic personnel and their issues. So long as there are no safety or legal reasons that demand immediate attention, chairs may be able to wait out a problematic personnel until they retire, change their behavior, or leave on their own.

- *Isolation.* It may be a useful tactic to isolate a difficult faculty or staff member so that the circle of those infected is minimized. The fewer people the person comes in contact with, the fewer may be hurt by that toxic person.

- *Transfer.* Can you arrange a transfer of the problem faculty or staff member to some other appropriate unit? Although it is unethical to unload your unit's problems onto some unsuspecting group, it is in everyone's best interests if talents are taken advantage of and the exhibition of personal difficulties is minimized.

22) *Response versus retaliation.* In the face of provocation or a situation caused by a problematic faculty or staff member, it may be appropriate to take action. Make sure that your response is designed and perceived to be a remedy and not a retaliation intended to hurt.

23) *Take the high ground.* Regardless of what problem personnel do or say, always try to take the moral high ground. This position helps clarify the next steps to take. Once your time as leader of your department ends, it will also be much easier for you to look at yourself in the mirror and say, "I did everything I could, the way I should."

24) *Analyze the coalitions.* Everyone has friends, and even those who are enemies on some issues can be collaborators under certain conditions. Even problematic personnel will have their supporters. Determine who they are because you may be able to work with them to remedy the situation. Or you may have to deal with them as well.

25) *In cases of racial or religious bias or sexual harassment, special rules apply.* Make sure that you consult with the dean and campus human resources on issues such as these since federal laws apply.

26) *A witness to discussions may be useful at times.* The witness can be a colleague, unbiased third party, union representative, clerical staff member, or human resources member. Sometimes a witness for both the administration and faculty or staff member may be present.

27) *Keeping the door open (literally).* It may be prudent to keep the office door open when meeting with a problem faculty or staff member. That way your conversations may be "witnessed" by office personnel, so that if a

charge is made against you for raising your voice or threatening, office staff can testify to the contrary. Having an open door may also be safer for you should conversations get too irate.

28) *Keeping the door open (symbolically).* Leaders need to remember that people and conditions change over time. Never completely close the door.

QUESTIONS TO CONSIDER

1) Think about one of the most challenging faculty you have ever dealt with. Put yourself in the place of the department chair. Write a list of four questions or comments that you would make. Also predict what that person would say in response.

2) Who on your campus would you see to talk to about a challenging faculty or staff member who has a substance abuse problem? Who could give you guidance so that you might help that faculty or staff member? Who could give you the legal advice that you need?

3) What are the tell-tale signs of substance abuse by a faculty or staff member?

4) Are you encouraged to take notes of meetings with problem personnel? What kind of notes would be most useful for a chair who wants to build a case for disciplinary action?

5) Have you been or do you know anyone who has been personally threatened by a challenging faculty or staff member? Describe the case. How was the case resolved?

12

Legal Considerations

It's been barely two months since Professor Sued became chair. Like all units of the university, this last round of budget reductions cut to the bone. With all of the easy money already gone from previous rounds, this last set of reductions will dig into the tenure-track lines and operating expenses essential to the Department of Mechanical Engineering. Dr. Pam Boxer, like all of the other recently hired assistant professors, is very concerned about her job. Although she was a prized catch from a recent national search, Dr. Boxer knows that her position is in jeopardy. She has already inquired of her union representative what special danger she may be in as the only nontenured woman on the faculty and since the specialty program for which she was hired, director of the women's engineering program, may itself be at risk. Dr. Boxer has asked for a meeting with the chair and has advised him that she wishes to bring her union representative along for this meeting. Professor Sued wants to be open and fair. At the same time, however, he wonders what he needs to do and say to protect the university and himself from legal threats.

From the safety of his lab, Professor Sued instructed and conducted his research in relative safety. So long as he followed established protocols for operating lab equipment, he had little to worry about. Now that he is department chair, however, Chair Sued needs to protect his faculty, department, university, and himself. Department chairs are the frontline officers charged with following due process and safeguarding the rights and obligations of individuals and the organization. Chairs are trustees of individual rights of the faculty, staff, and students. At the same time, however, they need to protect the university and themselves from unnecessary exposure to lawsuits. What do department chairs need to consider relative to the law?

1) *Chairs do not rule independently.* All faculty, students, staff, and administration are subject to the rules set forth in institutional bylaws, charters, faculty handbooks, student handbooks, local, state, and national laws, and the U.S. Constitution.

2) *Be aware of the perceptions of those with whom you communicate.* Unless justified, avoid statements that might be perceived as promissory. For example, do not say "Chances are you'll get the position," unless you know that that person will be offered the position. Most chair decisions are subject to approval by the dean and/or central administration.

3) *Generally, the courts act with judicial restraint relative to potential legal issues in the college or university.* This means that the courts usually do not look to get involved in higher education controversies. As professionals, we are given the opportunity to govern ourselves and to resolve controversies.

4) *It is expected that officers of the institution will act reasonably and in good faith.*

5) *The chance of a successful personal or individual liability judgment against a department chair is generally remote,* apart from egregious behavior outside of the department chair position's normal scope of conduct.

6) *Never act outside of the scope of your responsibilities as department chair.* Although you may be concerned with the personal lives of department members, chairs should not become involved unless personal matters begin to directly impact faculty or staff performance.

7) *Exercise good judgment and always try to act in the best interests of the department and institution* as you look out for the legal rights of those in the department. Motivation and intention are important legal considerations, as is preconceived intent to harm.

8) *Technological advances have opened new areas of legal interest to department chairs.*

- *Office computers typically owned by the institution are generally to be used solely for business purposes.* Does your institution exempt online communication from being accessed for the purpose of institutional management?

- *Become familiar with your institution's policies concerning ownership of copyrights to intellectual property.* This includes ownership rights to distance education material.

9) *Generally, chairs acting within the scope of their duties as department managers will be offered legal protection by their institutions.* It is always the right of the individual, however, to determine if that representation is in his or her best interests.

10) *Many professional associations offer liability insurance.* This insurance may offer some protection from personal legal costs.

11) *Legal liability may result from actions proven to be:*

- *Arbitrary and capricious:* Were actions that were taken customary and similar to those taken under other circumstances, or were actions taken without apparent reason or appropriate motivation?

- *Breach of contract:* Were contractual rights and/or obligations violated?

- *Violation of constitutional rights* to due process, free speech and association, or property rights.

- *Discrimination or harassment* based on race, gender, or special needs.

- *Common-law liability:* Was there a breach of duty to care for the safety and well-being of those for whom the chair is responsible? Was there a fraudulent misrepresentation or defamation of character?

12) *What should chairs consider as safeguards against legal problems?*

- *The best means of avoiding legal problems is to ensure that they do not occur in the first place.* Resolve issues when they are small so that they do not become larger problems.

- *Be crystal clear in communications* with department members and superiors and be able to provide evidence that you made every effort to communicate clearly.

- *Know the legal rights and responsibilities of those in your department,* as well as the protections and rights that you have as a representative of the institution.

- *Be familiar with the details of the critical policy documents* that you will need to refer to when dealing with sensitive personnel issues. Chairs should be intimately familiar with critical personnel contracts and policy provisions.

- *At the first hint of legal problems, communicate* with your dean, human resources, and legal counsel, should it be available to you on campus.

- *Consult with the best chairs on campus* to get multiple perspectives on difficult issues so that actions may be taken from an informed basis.

13) *Procedure, procedure, procedure.* The courts are very concerned with individual rights as they are protected by personnel review procedures. Make sure that deadlines are met, the required documents and reports are turned in, and the correct signatures appear.

14) *Be a good citizen; act in good faith and in the best interests of the department and institution.*

QUESTIONS TO CONSIDER

1) In reference to the scenario presented at the beginning of this chapter, if you were Chair Sued,

   • Would you permit the union representative to attend the meeting with Dr. Boxer?

   • Would you take comprehensive notes of who said what?

   • What would you say in response to Dr. Boxer's charge that she was being discriminated against due to her gender?

2) What would you do if you were given incorrect information by your dean, information that might expose you to legal liability?

3) How well does your institution protect chairs from legal liability?

13

PROFESSIONAL DEVELOPMENT

Professor Growing is the new chair of the Department of Public Policy. His predecessor was reactive relative to professional development. In other words, she waited for faculty to come to her with some proposal and then would see if there were any resources available to support that proposal. At times, this meant that anyone late with a request would not have money available since all the money had already been allocated. At times, this even meant that a presentation proposal that had been accepted to a conference in the late spring could not be supported, or there was no money available to support a grant-writing opportunity because the cupboard was bare. In recent years, the university empha- sized the importance of research publication but did not match its emphasis with new money to support research. This was especially a big problem for junior faculty, for whom research productivity was essential for tenure. Chair Growing recognizes the problem and is determined to ameliorate it by reallocating resources within the department. He is unwilling to accept the proposition that a lack of new money for scholar- ship is rationale for a lack of professional development support.

Professor Growing has now been chair for five years. Two years into his second term, he has made major changes to the professional develop- ment culture in the Department of Public Policy. Since he was active in the state professional organization, Chair Growing used his influence to gain a position on the advisory board for a legislative initiative to improve the quality of education for those going into the rural and small cities planning specialization. In this position he was privy to how the RFP was going to be written requesting grant proposals for innovative training initiatives. Professor Young is a new assistant professor recently hired in Chair Growing's department. She has carefully read materials passed to her by the chair and prepared a pilot training program for rural and small cities planners. This past summer a small training institute was funded using department seed money. Professor Young is well prepared to respond to the formal request for proposals coming out during the second year of her probationary appointment. She has a demonstrated track record of success in rural and small city planning, an advisory board already in place, is making improvements to assessment based on feedback from summer participants and already has enthusiastic buy-in from her local government agencies and legislators. Professor Young's graduate students staffed the summer institute and are preparing to present their model program at professional meetings and write it up for publication. She feels optimistic about her major grant application.

Chair Growing inherited a department development culture typical in many academic units. Although the previous administration did not consciously work to impede the professional development of the faculty, the net result was that faculty did not grow in their scholarship, teaching, and service as they might have had there been a chair who worked proactively to help the faculty match talents with opportunities. In Chair Growing's second term, he positioned himself so that he could help his junior faculty member both serve the department's service responsibilities and jump-start her career by putting her in a favorable position to gain a grant that promises to hold scholarly opportunities as well. Few if any will know what the chair has done for his junior faculty member. Justifiably, she will receive the credit for grant work and presentations and publications that may come from that work. But Chair Growing knows he has done what he should to serve his faculty.

The position of department chair is a service position. Perhaps the most satisfying part of chairing is helping colleagues grow in their scholarship, teaching, and service. While much of the chair role requires management of issues, budgets, schedules, and crises, it also makes it possible to arrange time and money and to provide the information that facilitates professional growth. Chairs have position power that places them at the locus of communication with internal and external constituents of potential benefit to faculty and staff. Chairs can also guide faculty in institutional and departmental directions so as to encourage professional work that benefits both the individual faculty and the academic unit. What should chairs consider relative to professional development?

1) *Department chairs are typically reactive or proactive relative to professional development.* Chairs who are reactive wait for faculty to forward proposals for a paper or some scholarly activity requiring financial support. The chair then decides if there is enough money to fund the proposal. Proactive chairs look for opportunities for the faculty to use their expertise, elicit the support of the faculty, and then develop a working plan, schedule, and budgets to support professional growth activities.

2) *Professional development requires resources, and it is the chair's responsibility to maximize those resources.* Typically, major corporations try to earmark at least 5% of their total budgets toward capital investment. How much of your department budget is earmarked for the growth and development of its most important productive capital—the faculty? A chair of a department with 10 full-time equivalent faculty may have a total budget of $1 million. Is the chair able to invest at least $50,000 for professional growth? In these tough budget times, if a chair is able to set aside even 2% of the total budget and earmark that 2% for professional development, it could be tremendously beneficial to the faculty.

3) *Develop a calendar of scheduled professional development events to help engender a professional development culture.* Faculty need to sense a quality of growth opportunities and a quantity of opportunities sufficient to help them stay at the forefront of their fields. As you try to keep up with the pace of change, it is important that department faculty and staff come to assume they are expected to grow professionally and that this growth will be supported by the department financially, politically, and socially. A faculty position without professional growth is a dead end. Departments

that embrace change and support professional growth are exciting places to come to work every day.

4) *The chair is responsible for encouraging the growth of all faculty in the department.* While junior faculty need assistance toward tenure and promotion, senior faculty also need support. Too often, professional growth is focused on assistant professors. A strong case can be made, however, that major support is needed for professional development even after promotion to full professor. Whereas junior faculty can mine their dissertations for discrete publishable pieces, senior faculty may be more prepared to write synthetical pieces with wide-ranging implications. These macro-level works and ground-breaking pieces require at least as much support as smaller pieces typically produced during the early stages of the professor's career.

5) *Meet individually with faculty to better understand their perception of their work, career stage, and direction.* Ask how the department can help, and show them how they can best develop themselves professionally to benefit the department as well as themselves. Colleges and universities are human places. Individuals each have their own history and their own motivations. The chair who successfully helps faculty develop over the long term will gear the department's professional growth efforts in recognition of the individual motivations of the faculty and staff.

6) *An approximate level of travel funding needs to be allocated one year before the presentation of a conference paper.* It is not enough to tell faculty that they will "probably" have travel funding "if" their submission for paper presentation is successful. Especially for a relatively lowly paid assistant professor, it is important that they know that if they put their valuable time into preparing a paper for presentation, and if their paper is accepted, then their trip to present will be affordable without unduly dipping into their meager personal or family resources. And so long as faculty have a general understanding of approximately how much they will have available for professional travel each year, they can then tentatively plan their paper presentation schedule with the reasonable assurance that their department will support their work. Such socio-emotional support tells

faculty that the department cares enough about them as scholars to put its money behind them.

7) *Student assistants can be of tremendous help to faculty.* Among the tasks they can assist with are conducting literature searches, copying, drafting documents, preparing for class, and grading, thus allowing faculty to fully employ their training and expertise rather than getting bogged down in clerical work. Student assistants are typically department majors who will also use their experiences in their resumes.

8) *Allocate funds for staff training as well as professional development.* The ever-changing software and hardware that faculty use necessitates the allocation of resources for staff training.

9) *Professional development can occur at national meetings attended by a few faculty, or consultants/distinguished professors can be brought to campus for workshops or seminars.* On-campus seminars of this type may be a much better bang for the buck. Professional development of this type is a cost-efficient means of promoting faculty growth and it serves social and political purposes by bringing institutional constituencies together on behalf of the department.

10) *Is there enough department consensus to permit an internal sabbatical program* whereby faculty volunteer to teach an additional section so that they can earn enough credits to warrant an extra sabbatical term?

11) *Subscribe to the* Chronicle of Higher Education. Have it on display in the department office and discuss issues of importance to the academy. By so doing, "specialists" who typically toil in isolation are connected to the universe of higher learning.

12) *Professional development includes promotion of faculty growth as a member of the institutional community.* Invite campus administrators to your department to discuss specific issues. These campus officers might include the president, provost, financial officer for academic affairs, the dean, and even the vice presidents for business administration and student affairs. It is good for the faculty's wider perspective, and it's good for department public relations.

13) *Seed money can be helpful to faculty applying for grants and fellowships.* Seed money can be used by faculty to help them pay for literature searches, drafting, and editing.

14) *Keep professional development alive in department meetings and in the halls.* Promote discussion and accolades for those who are actively involved in professional growth.

QUESTIONS TO CONSIDER

1) Who are some of the department chairs on your campus who have proactively facilitated the professional development of their faculty and staff? How have they done this?

2) In your department, what percentage of the total funds spent this year will have been allocated for professional development of faculty?

3) How much do chairs on your campus receive for their own professional development as department managers and leaders?

4) Describe the process that faculty go through to apply for funds for professional travel. Can any of the steps you have identified be eliminated or simplified?

5) Are the professional development needs of full professors treated the same way as are the needs of assistant professors?

6) You have been told by the dean that you may reallocate all of the funds that would have been paid for the salary of a full professor who will go on unpaid leave this year. How will you best use $80,000 for the professional development of your department members?

14

WORKLOAD CONSIDERATIONS

After following a lock-step formulaic model for workload assignments in the past, department chairs under a new academic vice president have been given greater freedom to flexibly adjust workload. Dr. Yihtza Burden is chair of the Department of Foreign Languages. She has been charged by the dean to look at the faculty workload in her department to determine whether teaching loads should be adjusted. Under the new scheduling format, faculty may be assigned one to four courses per term, so long as other assignments such as scholarship, committees, and other special assignments justify the teaching course load. She asks herself these questions: How do large jumbo classes compare to small seminar classes? How much does one regional committee chair position relate to membership on a prestigious national association board? How do a few discrete refereed publications compare to one large writing project that promises to synthesize a great deal of literature in linguistics? What is comparable workload?

Department chairs usually have to approve the unit's workload. Workload most directly refers to the teaching schedule. But the time not scheduled for teaching indirectly speaks to institutional expectations for research and other scholarly activities, committee assignments, and extraordinary service such as leading an accreditation effort. Abstractions such as educational philosophy, vision, and mission statements are operationalized by the chair's decisions as to the faculty who are chosen to teach, the scholarly work that is expected of faculty, and their other professional assignments. It is typically the department chair who must approve the courses faculty teach, and, if they are not teaching, what is expected of the faculty in the way of research, publications, grants, and the like. Strategic plans have to be actualized in the faculty workload.

For the most part, academic term teaching schedules and professional development expectations remain consistent. Most fall term teaching schedules resemble the schedule from the previous fall term. Unless there has been significant organizational change, expectations for scholarship, grant work, and service to the community and profession generally remain the same. When change is necessary, however, it is up to the department chair to make changes to faculty schedules and professional expectations. The department chair must work within the scope of union rules, campus policy, and department culture to actualize changes to improve or sustain the highest level of service to students while protecting the core mission of the department. When considering the faculty's workload, department chairs should think about the following.

1) *Is the class schedule in the best interests of the students and/or the faculty?* The teaching schedule is a political instrument in the sense that it is a public document that invites analysis and criticism. Senior faculty accustomed to teaching certain courses during particular time slots may feel a psychological ownership of the course and timeframe. But is this schedule in the best interests of the students? For example, are graduate courses taught at a time during the evening when it is convenient for working students to get to them? Are enough classes scheduled on Fridays to ensure student engagement rather than giving them an extra day to each weekend?

2) *Chairs are responsible for supporting faculty scholarship and service with the teaching schedule.* For example, are the scholarly faculty given large blocks of time in which to do their work? Does their teaching schedule allow them to serve the department in other ways such as in regularly scheduled faculty senate meetings or allow them the commute time necessary to observe student teaching?

3) *Should the current year's class schedule and faculty assignments follow the same schedule and assignments from last year?* For the most part new academic terms resemble the term from the previous year. Fall 2006 will resemble fall 2005. Most chairs will receive a copy of the previous year's teaching schedule to serve as the basis for the upcoming academic year's schedule. Unless the chair specifically changes the schedule, the former year's schedule will become the upcoming year's schedule. If certain classes have always been offered during one time slot, don't be surprised if students become upset with the change. They may have planned their work and study schedules around that historical time slot—especially if the course is a graduation requirement with a limited number of available seats.

4) *Chairs typically make changes to the schedule in two periods.* During the first period, chairs make the majority of changes during the regular scheduling period, which is typically six months before the onset of each academic term. The second scheduling period takes place at the beginning of the academic term. During the week before and the first week of class, events such as family emergencies, unexpected research opportunities or faculty leaves, budget crises, or unanticipated demand for specific sections may require the chair to juggle schedules as classes are about to begin.

5) *Who will draft the new schedule and faculty assignments?* In small departments, it is typically the chair who handles all of the scheduling. In larger departments of 20–40 faculty, however, it may be the associate chair or scheduling committee that develops a draft for the chair to consider.

6) *Is there a department agenda that needs to be addressed?* Agendas may include shifting the proportion of WTUs (weighted teaching units) devoted to programs, shifting WTUs to or away from temporary, part-time faculty and graduate students, class size reduction or increase, reduced load for probationers, load adjustments based on research faculty needs or buyouts, enhanced professional development needs for certain faculty or class of faculty, increasing or reducing laboratory requirements, enhancing or diminishing graduate or certificate programs, increasing or decreasing WTUs devoted to electives, general education, or high FTES sections.

7) *Are there special assignments that will further the department agenda that need to be balanced by reduced workload for certain faculty?* Special assignments may include a lengthy accreditation report, development, grant work, curriculum or new course development, and community service.

8) *Is there department consensus on workload priorities?* A change in courses taught and when they are taught should be discussed privately with the affected faculty before changes are made public. Similarly, changes in scholarly expectations warrant discussion so that they are not a surprise to the faculty.

9) *What is the legal range of workload assignment? What is the historical cultural workload?* In a unionized faculty, there are typically limits to the number of units that can be taught. This unit teaching maximum may vary for tenure-track faculty as opposed to nontenure-track faculty. Service in the way of committee work is often counted as a significant portion of the faculty's workload. In some systems, it is even possible to forgo committee work by teaching an extra section. Relative to historical culture, departments vary as to expectations for teaching and scholarship. In many departments, little committee work is expected of new probationary faculty as they get their teaching and research up to speed. New faculty may even receive a reduced teaching load to help them move toward tenure. Senior full professors are often expected to produce the most original, far-reaching scholarship and chair the most important influential committees.

10) *Are the same rooms and facilities available?* Strategic planning and vision sound grand, but a large part of the chair's work is less glamorous. For example, it is critical for department planning purposes that rooms are available with necessary seat capacities. If, for example, large-enrollment courses have 100 seats available to them instead of the last term's 200 seats, that small change could lead to a department crisis in enrollments. Or if an unmediated classroom is substituted for a full-mediated room, that could have significant impact on the quality of the course that can be taught. It is important that chairs know who makes decisions about what rooms will be available for instruction and when those decisions are made.

11) *Are there technologies available in certain facilities that will help deliver instruction?* Distance technology can deliver instruction anywhere in the world. New software allows all students to respond to the professor's question rather than just the first student to raise his or her hand. Even low-tech can significantly alter the delivery of courses for the better. For example, can a number of smaller classrooms be linked to one instructor who can then teach multiple sections simultaneously?

12) *Have faculty been asked for suggestions as to how they might want their schedules changed?* It is wise practice to ask for schedule suggestions from the faculty prior to the deadline for submission of such changes to the administration. Chairs should also provide time for discussion in the event of controversial changes to the schedule.

13) *Is every section of the teaching schedule absolutely required?* Is the schedule the way it is because of history, culture, or some admission to convenience?

QUESTIONS TO CONSIDER

1) In your department, how well does the schedule fit the needs of the students and the desires of the faculty? Explain your answer.

2) In your department, what is the mix of classes relative to enrollment? How many sections are there with enrollments greater than 100, 99–50, 49–20, 19–10, less than 10?

3) What are the largest rooms on your campus available for jumbo sections? In the event of conflicts between departments that want to schedule those rooms at the same hours, who gets scheduling priority and on what basis is priority determined?

4) What is the legal minimum and maximum for faculty to teach? What is the "normal" teaching load? Is there consensus as to when "normal" teaching loads are not applicable? Explain your responses.

5) If your department had a 5% reduction in its personnel budget, what would you delete, combine, or add to the teaching schedule? What changes would you make in the event of a 10% reduction?

15

How to Support Teaching and Learning

A great deal has happened at Southernmost University in the last 30 years. Enrollments have grown the student body from 6,000 to 12,000. Large numbers of minority students have taken advantage of inexpensive tuition and the university's reputation as an excellent teaching institution. President Gash has been able to negotiate agreements with the state legislature to ensure minimally acceptable levels of funding to date. However, this is about to change. All departments have been told that they must redouble their research, grant, and contract efforts so that Southernmost can keep up with rising demands on its resources. The senior faculty are resistant to this change. The junior faculty want to be left alone so that they can publish and get tenured. The faculty use accreditation and general education as reasons not to dramatically change how or what they teach. During department meetings, the cry is often heard, "Remember the good old days when teaching mattered?" Dr. Learner is chair of the Department of Psychology. In his 12 years at Southernmost he has seen the pendulum swing from an emphasis on teaching to external funding efforts and then back again to teaching and learning. He is a strong advocate of good teaching but he wonders how he should go about supporting teacher-centered learning, what exactly it is, how to measure it, and how to weigh it against scholarship and grant/contract work.

In organizational research, a very important question is *cui bono*—who is the primary beneficiary? If colleges and universities are to most benefit students, clearly, chairs need to support better teaching. How can department chairs support the highest quality teaching in their departments and fit it within the political and budget realities of higher education?

1) *Have regular discussions about the definition of good teaching.* Is good teaching mostly memorization of fundamental facts? Application of theory? Higher-order thinking and creativity? Can good teaching be assessed objectively through pass rates on national standardized tests, or through student evaluations, faculty observations, and/or grade distributions?

2) *Support professional development efforts aimed at improving teaching.* Too often sabbaticals and assigned time are only spent on research and publication. Why not focus sabbaticals on the improvement of instruction? The tangible evidence of a well-spent sabbatical is a revised, improved course outline and lesson plans.

3) *Allocate student assistants to faculty to help them improve their teaching.* Students might research similar courses on the web and in sister institutions so that the faculty can know what course outlines contain, the resources that are being employed, and even the subjects covered by colleagues teaching similar courses.

4) *Post all syllabi on the web so that colleagues can see the good work the department is doing.*

5) *Routinely schedule a teaching briefing where selected faculty highlight what they are doing in their courses.* This invites discussion and suggestions and improves interdepartmental communications.

6) *Schedule meetings of faculty teaching linked courses.* Set up meetings of faculty whose courses feed into other courses or are fed into by instructors teaching preliminary courses. In this way, faculty are kept up to date as to what they need to teach in order to best support each other. It also builds a pedagogical community of faculty with similar academic interests.

7) *Encourage team teaching and teaching between members of different departments.* Cross-fertilization can revitalize teaching and complement pedagogical styles.

8) *Send teams of faculty to conferences that focus on pedagogy.* Have these faculty present a workshop highlighting what they have learned to their colleagues.

9) *Schedule student assistants to routinely videotape teaching* so that faculty can review their own work.

10) *Schedule some of your best students to take notes in classes so that faculty can see the students' perception of what is being taught.* By checking a good student's notes, faculty can come up with ways to more clearly get their messages across.

11) *During exit interviews with graduating students, ask them what courses were most valuable, what courses were least valuable, and how each might be improved.* Relay this information appropriately to instructors for their consideration.

12) *Regularly review courses.* Appoint the department curriculum committee or some other group to look at course syllabi, materials, and other indicators of course content on a regular basis. Courses chosen for review might be all those in a certain major focus area or courses at a certain undergraduate or graduate level. Regardless of who teaches a course and how long they have taught it, a collegial set of eyes looking at a course every three to five years can give instructors fresh ideas.

13) *Discuss the improvement of teaching in department meetings.* The chair's management of department meeting agendas provides a wonderful opportunity to talk about what is important to the department. Why not highlight the superior teaching of faculty whose good pedagogical ideas might benefit some of their colleagues?

QUESTIONS TO CONSIDER

1) How important is teaching in your department compared to scholarship and service?

2) In your department, how is adequate teaching recognized as different from superior teaching?

3) Is there a difference in the quality of teaching possible in a class of 100 students as opposed to a class of 400 students?

4) If your department was faced with the need to reduce personnel expenses by 20%, what course sections could you combine? Defer to next term? To next year? Temporarily substitute for some other major requirement? Revise syllabi so as to meet multiple major requirements within one course?

16

CHAIR-DEAN RELATIONS

Associate Professor Joyner has just been elected chair of the Department of Music. The department has three tenured, two probationary, and eight part-time faculty. Chair Joyner is the third chair in five years. This is a problematic time in the College of Humanities and Fine Arts, of which music is one of seven departments. The college hopes its new dean, the third in the last five years, will bring stability to an uncomfortably fluid political situation. Dean Strong is 59 years old and has extensive leadership experience at a similar comprehensive university in the Midwest, having worked as associate dean in charge of financial planning, grants, and contracts. In the remainder of the university, departments have been merged, reduced, and eliminated. Dr. Tyght, who was hired as provost one year ago, has told Dean Strong that the departments in the College of Humanities and Fine Arts must develop a plan to preserve resources and find direction consistent with the trustees' demand that the budget be balanced and nonviable programs be reduced or eliminated. Professor Joyner will meet with the new dean and her colleagues during a college leadership retreat. She is scheduled for a one-hour personal orientation with the dean to present her department's strengths and weaknesses, and she will also be asked for her plan for the future directions for her unit.

In the rapidly changing university and college environment, such a scenario is not uncommon. Since deans do not typically reside next door to department members or have daily interaction with faculty from one department, the small amounts of time that chairs spend with deans is critical for the welfare of that department. How the chair represents the department, what chairs say and do, the problems from departments that appear on the dean's desk or that walk through the door will have a direct impact on how the dean perceives the department's faculty, staff, and students and its productivity and influence. Before meeting with the dean, what should Chair Joyner bear in mind?

Deans are middle-level management just like chairs. While chairs may officially still be faculty, or partly administration, deans are officially administration. Their overview extends to multiple departments and programs. They are usually charged with transmitting the directives and directions of the vice president for academic affairs and the president and seeing to it that those directions are translated, as much as possible, into the most effective programs at the department level. Deans officially are appointed to their positions by these central administrators. And while college faculty are typically given the opportunity to provide input into the dean's periodic job evaluations, deans are more responsible to the president and vice president for academic affairs than they are to chairs and faculty of the departments in the dean's college. Deans can be relieved of their positions by central administration only. Deans also receive a budget allocation from the vice president for academic affairs that deans then allocate to departments in the college.

1) *Chairs need to make sure that the dean is familiar with the discipline as well as the department.* While some deans will have experience with all of the disciplines in their colleges, others will not, or they will have preconceptions about a discipline that are inaccurate. A good way of educating the dean, along with the department faculty, is to regularly invite the dean to department meetings and functions. Deans also need an overview of the faculty in the department, their strengths and weaknesses, and what they can do and cannot do.

2) *Carefully consider the best way to handle faculty who speak directly to the dean about internal department matters.* The culture of openness and accessibility common on most campuses means that just about any faculty

member can speak directly to any administrator, but what is the purpose behind the communication? Is the faculty member trying to go over the chair's head, run around the chair or a department committee, or circumvent a department decision? Deans can support the chair by asking the faculty member if he or she has spoken to the chair first and then briefing the chair about the meeting. Or deans can undermine the chair's authority by dealing directly with faculty and not work through the chair or department governance structures.

3) *A chair who tries to go above the head of the dean is asking for someone's head to roll*—either their own or someone else's. If a chair must communicate directly with a dean's superior, it is in the chair's and the department's best interests to inform the dean that it is going to happen and the reasons for the communication.

4) *Credibility is important for both the dean and the chair.* Both should know that the other will do as they say they will do, that they mean what they say, and that the information provided is accurate.

5) *Chairs need to realize that administrative decisions require timely information.* If a dean asks for information, chairs need to provide that information by requested deadlines.

6) *Chairs need to understand the political, economic, and social environment in which the dean operates.* The larger the number of people affected by decisions, the more interests are involved. Letting the dean know that the chair understands the complexity and difficulty of decisions lends support to the dean.

7) *Chairs should try to understand their dean well enough so that they can make accurate, educated guesses as to how the dean will interpret and react to various scenarios.*

8) *How much of what the dean says is coming directly from above?* Some deans will make a decision as to how to "adjust" the message that they have received from their superiors. Others will take their marching orders directly and relay them as they have been given to them. Not all messages from above can be applied uniformly across all departments throughout an institution. Some deans see it as their responsibility to interpret what they are told to say; other deans just relay the message.

9) *What is the dean's agenda?* What does the dean envision for the college? What would the dean want college departments to look like in the way of courses, research, grant and contract work, and service to the community and campus?

10) *Information is critical.* Finding out what a decision is and why it was made is important for understanding the decision and helps to accurately predict what might happen in the future. Chairs who are credible, trustworthy, and confidential are more likely to receive timely information than chairs who do not have the confidence of the dean. In addition, if chairs discover information of potential value to the dean, the dean will be very appreciative of information that allows them to be more effective.

11) *Deans hope that chairs will handle most or all of the problems in the department* without having to involve them too often. The very worst situation for deans is to learn about a problem in their own college from the academic vice president and be told to fix it.

12) *Deans want to hear good news much more than they want to hear bad news.* Too often deans only deal with problems. Chairs need to make sure that the dean also knows about awards received by the faculty and students, significant publications and research accolades, good works for constituent groups, and the like.

13) *Good information about the department is symbolic capital* that can be used by the dean to speak on behalf of the department's interests.

14) *How does the dean perceive relations should be between departments in the college?* Are departments competing for resources or are they collaborating to maximize resource utilization?

15) *Is the dean also the budget officer for the college, or is there someone else* in the office who drafts allocations and constructs reports for the dean to review and approve? If someone else in the office is charged with staffing budget operations, chairs need to know that person well.

16) *What primary accounting metrics does the dean use to oversee efficient utilization of resources?* Is it student head count? Number of student credit units produced? Full-time equivalent enrollments? Student-faculty ratios? Number of small sections? Number of jumbo-size sections? Cost in

dollars for each student taught? Knowing the primary metrics used by the dean informs chairs how efficiency of resources is determined. It will help the chair know if the dean perceived the department as effective, efficient, and productive.

17) *Never surprise the dean.* Chairs need to make certain that their dean is prepared to receive news about what is going on in the department. A dean who learns of a negative incident that happened in the college from another dean or central administrator is an unhappy dean. The appearance is that the dean does not know what is going on in his or her own house.

18) *Deans depend on chairs to draft schedules and make decisions about most allocations within their departments.* The success of a dean depends upon how well chairs and their departments do their work. Rarely does a dean have the time or energy to micromanage departments. Chairs need to remember, however, that the dean typically has the power to withhold approval of most schedules and expenditures. Extraordinary chair decisions should be explained before they reach the dean's desk.

19) *Chairs who want freedom to act on behalf of their departments should expect to be held accountable and responsible for their actions.* For example, chairs who would like the freedom to move budget allocations from personnel to professional development allocations need to make sure that major, general education, and other course requirements are satisfied.

QUESTIONS TO CONSIDER

1) Analyze your department from the dean's point of view. Analyze some other department in your college from the dean's point of view.

2) Take the perspective of the vice president for academic affairs and analyze your college compared to other colleges on your campus.

3) What are the three best pieces of good news coming from your department? Does your dean know about these?

4) Would it be a good idea to invite the dean to one of your department meetings? If so, what should be on the agenda?

5) How do the deans on your campus handle appointments made by faculty to discuss internal department affairs?

6) What major issues are brewing in your department? How aware is the dean of these impending problems?

7) If your dean invited you to present a case that gives you the authority to reallocate personnel dollars, what arguments would you make?

8) What evidence can a chair present to demonstrate the effective use of budgeted dollars?

9) What drives your dean? What is on his or her agenda?

PART III

LEADING, MANAGING, AND CHANGING THE ACADEMIC DEPARTMENT

THE DEPARTMENT CHAIR AS MANAGER AND LEADER

Begin with the end in mind.
—Stephen Covey, *The Seven Habits of Highly Effective People*

It is often fashionable for department members to skeptically approach the idea of someone managing the work of the faculty. The academic culture is much more sympathetic to the needs of faculty autonomy than the needs of the administration for accounting controls to manage resources, programs, and measures of academic productivity. But the new realities of public and private higher education now require careful management of academic departments. As bureaucracies have been pared down to reduce administrative overhead, both management and leadership responsibilities have been passed to the department level. The flattening of the bureaucratic pyramid now means that departments have more responsibilities than ever. Citizens and consumers demand accountability. Competition for dollars, the best students, and faculty positions is fierce. When the academic department was first institutionalized as the primary organizing structure for faculty, colleges were small and management happened in the central administration building. Today, however, departments need chairs able and willing to lead, to provide new opportunities for their faculty and students, and to fulfill their responsibilities as trustees of the department's future.

113

For faculty and staff to do their best work, chairs need to be effective managers as well as leaders of their academic departments. It is not enough by itself to want to be a leader. Before chairs can be in position to jump out front, they need to know what they have behind them; that is, what they have to work with. What are the givens? What are the assets and liabilities that they have to work with and within? What will they have to manage? And what is management?

MANAGEMENT

Management is the effective use and coordination of resources to achieve predefined objectives. To manage, chairs must plan, organize, and control all available resources such as capital, plant, materials, and labor to achieve defined objectives with maximum efficiency. Given a prescribed mission, organizational policies, structures and procedures, department chairs as managers plan, coordinate, and supervise the use of already allocated resources to achieve an established department mission.

Effective management is a required precondition for department success. As chief administrators of their departments, chairs need to be competent managers. Chairs need to be familiar with the following:

- The strategic plan for their institutions, colleges, and department

- The institution's important policies, significant data sources, and the documents that contain information used for planning and assessment

- Who to see for information critical for efficient department management

- What they have available in the way of resources (budget allocations, personnel and their competencies, facilities and equipment, curriculum and schedule)

The bottom line is that before chairs can lead their departments to significant positive change, they need to be competent managers of what they have. Once they are effective managers, chairs have the opportunity to lead their departments to greater achievements. What is leadership?

LEADERSHIP

Leadership is the art of creating an environment and influencing people to willingly follow a chosen direction. It requires a clear vision, visible values, and high expectations that guide members of the organization along a path that realizes the vision. Leaders have the skill to help people do a better job through coaching, facilitating, and by creating environments that serve the organization's members. Chairs as leaders understand critical institutional processes, they know the key institutional players, they are able to remove organizational roadblocks that hinder the faculty's natural tendency to produce quality, and they empower faculty and staff to achieve organizational goals consistent with their own talents and motivations. Chairs who are leaders have the opportunity to forge new directions for the department. The leader is less bound by prescribed circumstances of resources and existent operationalizations of the department mission and preexisting expectations for the level of possible faculty achievement. In difficult times leaders bolster their units from falling further than they need to. In favorable times, leaders shoot for some place better than where they already are.

One of the most simple yet sound pieces of advice Stephen Covey (1989) provides future leaders is "begin with the end in mind" (p. 95). For department chairs, this means that all of the preparation and transformation of concepts and philosophy into policy, program, and action needs to begin with a clear idea as to what a model department should look like, feel like, stand for, how people should behave, and what everyone in the organization should try to help it achieve. If leaders are able to vividly portray their vision of what the department should look like and powerfully paint this image in the minds of faculty, staff, and students, then all members of the organization will have the same direction for their actions, big and small. In Covey's mind, the first, most essential task of leaders is to so powerfully and consistently paint an image of what the organization should look like at the end that it convinces group members of the importance of this end. Then members of the organization will feel compelled to move the group forward in a self-directed fashion.

What is the best department that you know? What makes it so good? Is it distinctive in some way? What would have to be done to your department to emulate the best department you know? What does the best department you know of feel like in the halls? What is its climate like? Does its faculty and staff profile resemble your department? How is that department positioned politically on and off campus? How does your budget look compared to that exemplary department's budget? Is the same proportion allocated for operating expenses? For tenure-track and temporary personnel? How is performance counseling handled? How much professional development goes on there? How much does the faculty get to support their work? How good is the teaching in that distinctive department? What would a chair have to do to make his or her own department the best teaching department on campus? Gone are the days when chairs could depend on central administration to make their departments better. It's now up to them.

CHANGING THE ACADEMIC DEPARTMENT

When Northernmost University was only 3,000 students, it seemed that faculty and administration knew all of their colleagues personally. State funding was predictable and steady. Demographic and fiscal changes, however, have been paralleled by rapid changes in central administration and enrollment pressures that have increased the student population to 9,000 in 10 years. Three different deans have inhabited that office in the last six years. It used to be that faculty did their time as department chair and then rotated out. Much of the daily operation of the department was handled by the clerical staff who knew what to do based upon many, many years of observing how things had always been done. A don't-rock-the-boat culture was characteristic of most department faculty who saw chairs who tried to do too much as creating unnecessary problems. New legislative mandates to improve and prove the quality of education, with those mandates tied to continued funding, have shaken things up at Northernmost. Whereas the state used to provide 90% of the university's funds, in recent years that figure has been reduced to 80%, with the expectation that only 70% of the budget will be provided by the state in three years. Strategic planning, total quality management, and responsibility-based budgeting are all new concepts on this tradition-bound campus. Departments and colleges that have adapted

117

to these mandates appear to have been resourced better and been more favorably treated. What is a new chair to do in a department that continues to blame lack of administrative support for continuing to do as things have always been done?

Academic departments are resistant to change. For most faculty, the body of knowledge is what is important, and that body of knowledge changes only incrementally. Tenure ensures academic freedom and a level of self-governance almost unknown in contemporary society. But tenure also makes rapid change problematic. With more and more state-supported institutions vying with private institutions for scarce resources, the ability of academic organizations to change with shifting political and economic environments is becoming increasingly important to the viability of the college and university. Central administrators can preach the need for change in the institution, but it is at the department level where change must take place. While facing budget crises, political weakness, and social needs, departments must also deal with course schedule adjustments, faculty resources and programs that need shifting, external relations that need renewed emphasis, and the shift from teacher- to student-centered learning. How can chairs encourage change? Kotter (1996, p. 21) has developed a useful model that outlines the steps required for substantive changes in organizations.

1) Establish a sense of urgency.

2) Create the guiding coalition.

3) Develop a vision and strategy.

4) Communicate the change vision.

5) Empower broad-based action.

6) Generate short-term wins.

7) Consolidate gains and produce more change.

8) Anchor new approaches in the culture.

The first step requires that members of the organization understand the need for immediate action. Inertia needs to be overcome, and change needs to be perceived as more necessary than the benefit of doing nothing at all. Information presented in a persuasive fashion is needed to convince the faculty that change is urgent to the viability of all they have worked for.

Next, a guiding coalition needs to be formed. Membership of the coalition must be representative of the organization so that it has credibility. The coalition can make decisions and plan action necessary for change.

The coalition develops a vision for the end product of change that is so compelling that all of the organization's efforts to change move toward the realization of that vision. Once the vision has been established, a strategy for realization of that vision can be developed. A step-by-step game plan with timelines and metrics to document progress can inform the coalition that it is taking the right steps toward positive change.

Communication is the next step. By communicating the vision in a persuasive fashion, maximum group buy-in is obtained and opposition minimized. Models that are revised with input from constituent groups lead to a refined, sophisticated vision with buy-in from the overall organization. Diversity of opinions is valued and differences are respected as legitimate. The process is as important as the actual vision statement if human resources are to be maximized by a sense that the department is in this together.

After buy-in for the vision has been achieved, broad-based action is directed by the guiding coalition. By taking advantage of the talents and contacts of organizational members, change may be effected on many fronts. The change that comes from the efforts of few is not nearly as long lasting as that which comes from the actions of the faculty, staff, and student body. Once again buy-in is maximized. By acting to effect change, belief in the necessity for change is engendered.

The way the organization knows that it is making positive change is by identifying and then realizing short-term gains. If the decision has been made, for example, to bolster professional development funds for probationary faculty, it is easy to see that more assistant professors are getting research assistants, travel money, and seed money for grants. Small, concrete steps added together engender a sense of positive movement for the group as a whole.

Over the course of time, these small gains are consolidated, and they can become part of the department culture. A certain percentage of funds can be reserved to support new hires, for example. Over the course of several hires, this kind of professional development support can become a part of what it means to be a member of the department. The culture of the department changes when goals, values, behaviors, and emotional dispositions show continuity over the course of years and generations of administration.

QUESTIONS TO CONSIDER

1) On a scale from 1–5, with 1 = strongly disagree and 5 = strongly agree, respond to the following statements:

____ Chairs should primarily fulfill the wishes of their department faculty.

____ Chairs should serve only one term, then allow another faculty member to rotate into the position.

____ Chairs should proactively lead their departments by maximizing resources to their departments, efficiently allocating those resources to their faculty and staff, and seeking to align opportunities with the faculty best able to take advantage of those opportunities.

Share your answers with your peers. Why did you answer as you did?

2) How much of the department budget do you believe chairs should have the authority to allocate? Explain your response.

3) Are chairs on your campus encouraged to lead?

4) Are chairs on your campus given the information they need to manage their departments well?

5) Does your department want to be led? How much do faculty want to be left alone?

6) What obstacles to effective management and leadership do you face in your department?

7) How clear is your department's vision? Does your department have a mission statement? How close to your department's vision is its mission statement?

8) On your campus, who do chairs need to know well so they can manage and lead well?

9) What are the key documents that chairs on your campus need to know in order to manage and lead well?

10) Rate yourself on a scale from 1–5, with 1 = little leadership responsibility and 5 = a great deal of leadership responsibility. How much do you believe you have a responsibility to lead your department? Why have you answered as you have?

19

THE WINDS OF CHANGE AND DEPARTMENT OPERATIONS: A CASE STUDY

ENVIRONMENTAL SCAN

With an enrollment of 10,000 FTES, Oregon Northern University is part of a multi-campus state university system that has undergone extensive changes in recent years. Like many other public universities, ONU is no longer a state-supported institution but a state-assisted institution. Ninety percent of the university's operating expenses had been financed by the state 10 years ago, but today only 60% comes from the state general fund. It is expected that state revenues will drop another 10% over the next two years. With dwindling contributions from the legislature, the ONU Board of Trustees has given new university President Hu a mandate to find alternate sources of income and improve efficiency of operations. Raising tuition 40% over 10 years has helped balance accounts, but it has also reduced applications and enrollments.

THE DEPARTMENT OF ECONOMICS

The Department of Economics is located within the College of Social Sciences and primarily serves general education students. There are twelve faculty: six full professors, four newly hired assistant professors, and two part-time faculty. The normal teaching load for tenure-track faculty has historically been four classes per term, with an average section enrollment of twenty at the undergraduate level. Research has not been heavily weighted in tenure and promotion reviews.

With the retirement of his predecessor, Dr. Lee, an international studies expert, is now chair of the department. After no other faculty volunteered for the position, Dr. Lee was asked to consider serving as chair by Provost Gold, who was newly appointed to her position by President Hu after a national search. Dr. Lee is well liked by his department, respected for his scholarly achievements, and was endorsed through faculty vote. Last year, this productivity earned him promotion to full professor.

The department climate has been very comfortable. No substantive issues have been raised by the faculty, who have seen their job responsibilities change little over the 18-year tenure of the previous chair. General satisfaction with the status quo is reflected by infrequent faculty meetings. The department has enjoyed adequate funding for department operations, but there has been no funding allocated for professional development. To date, budget and fund disbursements have been centrally controlled, but the college's new administrator, Dean Steel, says that she is willing to consider greater department autonomy in return for a change in the department mission and operations. The Department of Economics, the College of Social Sciences, and the entire university have been directed by the trustees to enhance public visibility, external funding, and increase the efficiency of operations. Dean Steel has instructed all of her departments that they need to move in these directions or risk position shifts between departments in the college. With four senior faculty set to retire in the next three years, the Department of Economics is particularly vulnerable.

Violently opposed to change is Professor Ward, who has been in the department since earning his Ph.D. in 1974 and served as chair of the academic senate in 1991. He leads a group of three other senior faculty who oppose any change in department mission, priorities, or teaching load. Two of his supporters in the department chair the curriculum committee and the personnel committee. One other senior faculty, not as close to Professor Ward, is Professor Silver, who has recently returned to the department after six years as associate provost of academic affairs.

THE ISSUES BEFORE THE CHAIR

A number of issues face Chair Lee as he takes the department helm.

1) How should Chair Lee proceed with the dean's instructions? Should he support her directions? Explain your answer. Over the next few months, whom should he meet with and for what purpose?

2) What data and information does he need to collect? Outline a strategic and tactical plan for him to implement during the first year of his leadership and service.

3) Should the workload of junior faculty be reduced to two classes per term while they are directed to ramp-up their scholarship and grant work? If yes, what needs to be done to implement this change? How about the workload of the senior faculty? What options should be considered? If alterations to workload will be made, how should the chair go about implementing changes? Should he make assignments himself?

4) Assistant Professor Moneymaker's area is environmental economics. He is very strong in grant-work and highly recruited by prestigious land-grant universities. Should Chair Lee more strongly support Professor Moneymaker so as to retain his services? What should the chair do? What repercussions may result from the chair's actions?

5) Due to an announced retirement, Chair Lee must draft a vacancy description for the *Chronicle of Higher Education*. What should the advertisement say? How should Chair Lee proceed with the search?

6) How should Chair Lee advise the four assistant professors relative to the direction of the department? How should he counsel the senior faculty? What needs to be said to both sets of the faculty?

7) What strategies might Chair Lee employ to acquire the professional development funds that his four assistant professors need?

8) Chair Lee needs to develop his first budget proposal. This document is due in eight months. What data and information does he need to collect? Outline his proposed budget and be prepared to justify to the dean any expenditure projection.

9) Analyze the Department of Economics from the perspective of Dean Steel.

10) Chair Lee would like to initiate discussions as to the department's strategic plan in light of new institutional priorities. Develop a plan that he could employ during the first department meeting of the year. What topics should be considered? What background should be provided? Who should be on the agenda to speak? What problems should the chair anticipate? How much time should be provided for each phase of the agenda? What should be the tone of the meeting—Crisis mode? Upbeat and optimistic? Cool and objective?

11) The senior faculty have criticized Oregon Northern University's new direction by asserting that teaching will suffer. What options does the chair have to respond to this criticism?

ADDITIONAL RESOURCES

Academic Chairpersons Conference
http://www.dce.ksu.edu/academicchairpersons

Academic Leadership Consulting
Contact Don Chu at dchu@uwf.edu

American Council on Education Department Chair Online Resource Center
http://www.acenet.edu/resources/chairs/

American Council on Education Department Chair Workshops
http://www.acenet.edu/programs/dlp/

Harvard University Management Development Program
http://www.gse.harvard.edu/ppe/highered/programs/mdp.html

BIBLIOGRAPHY

Bolman, L. G., & Deal, T. E. (1997). *Reframing organizations: Artistry, choice, and leadership.* San Francisco, CA: Jossey-Bass.

Boyer, E. L. (1990). *Scholarship reconsidered: Priorities of the professoriate.* Princeton, NJ: Carnegie Foundation for the Advancement of Teaching.

Chu, D., & Veregge, S. (2002). *The California State University department chair survey report.* Retrieved July 21, 2005, from the California State University web site: http://www.calstate.edu/AcadSen/Records/Reports/CSU_Chairs_survey_report.pdf

Covey, S. R. (1989). *The seven habits of highly effective people.* New York, NY: Simon and Schuster.

Gmelch, W. H. (2000). *Department chair development.* Workshop presented at the American Council on Education Department Chair Workshops, San Diego, CA.

Hecht, I. W. D., Higgerson, M. L., Gmelch, W. H., & Tucker, A. (1999). *The department chair as academic leader.* Phoenix, AZ: American Council on Education/Oryx Press.

Higgerson, M. L. (1996). *Communication skills for department chairs.* Bolton, MA: Anker.

Kotter, J. P. (1996). *Leading change.* Boston, MA: Harvard Business School Press.

Robert, H. M., III, Evans, W. J., Honemann, D. H., & Balch, T. J. (2000). *Robert's rules of order* (10th ed.). New York, NY: Perseus.

Taylor, F. W. (1911). *The principles of scientific management.* New York, NY: Harper Brothers.

Index